— *the* —

SMART
FAMILY'S
PASSPORT

— the —

SMART
FAMILY'S

PASSPORT

350 MONEY, TIME &
SANITY SAVING TIPS

by **NINA WILLDORF** *and*
the **readers of BUDGET**
TRAVEL MAGAZINE

QUIRK BOOKS
PHILADELPHIA

Library of Congress Control Number: 2009934780

ISBN: 978-1-59474-448-8

Printed in China

Typeset in Bembo, Helvetica, OCRA, OCRB, and Trade Gothic

Designed by Doogie Horner and Steve DeCusatis
Production management by John J. McGurk

Distributed in North America by Chronicle Books
680 Second Street
San Francisco, CA 94107

10 9 8 7 6 5 4 3 2 1

Quirk Books
215 Church Street
Philadelphia, PA 19106
www.irreference.com
www.quirkbooks.com

CONTENTS < < < < < < < < < < < < < < <

Introduction

I thought I knew everything about how to travel like a pro—until I had a baby. The first time I found myself packing for a family getaway, the joke was on me. My wriggly little girl was hardly going to sail right through airport security and sleep her way across the country unless I had a couple of tricks up my sleeve. I started collecting ideas (pacifier clips! single-serving bags of formula!). But I was seriously put to shame once I looked to the *Budget Travel* readership—the savviest crew out there.

It takes the combined wisdom of hundreds of family travelers to truly ease the way. How else would you think to cover hotel electrical outlets with duct tape or remove sand with baby powder or claim the long-distance flier's saving grace: the bulkhead bassinet?

No one is happier than a parent who's nailed a surefire strategy to make family getaways go smoothly. This book, a collection of the smartest tips we've received from the readers of *Budget Travel* magazine, is full of such handy solutions. Two years ago, we published our general travel tips in *The Smart Traveler's Passport*. Since parents are some of the biggest collectors, and sharers, of smart strategies, *The Smart Family's Passport* was the natural next step.

We may have missed something that has made *your* family's life easier. So let us know what you have in your bag of tricks. Send us your best ones at Tips@BudgetTravel.com. If we run your find in the magazine, we'll give you a free subscription. The gratitude of your fellow travelers is just a bonus.

NINA WILLDORF

Editor in Chief

Budget Travel and BudgetTravel.com

CHAPTER ONE

BUDGET TRAVEL

01

PREPARE FOR TAKEOFF:

PLANNING A FAMILY TRIP

CHEAT SHEET If you get brochures from a family-travel out-fitter, stash them away—even if you don't plan on taking one of the trips. The literature usually includes great ideas for hotels and excursions that will come in handy later, when you plan your own vacation.

Chris Barker, Kingsport, Tenn.

ALL-INCLUSIVE ITINERARY To get my teenagers excited about a trip, I ask each of them to research where we're going and to come up with some group activities. Along the way, we've been treated to a tour of a Civil War battlefield and a cannonball contest in the pool.

Deb Kushnick, Marietta, Ga.

10

The Smart Family's Passport

ACT OUT In the weeks before my husband and I took our children, then ages 4, 8, and 14, on a three-week tour of Europe, we played banker and pretended to exchange dollars for euros and pounds (great math lesson). We also staged theme dinners, and when I attempted to make paella, we spoke only Spanish at the table.

Ashleigh Briant-Hodges, Orinda, Calif.

CARD TRICK When planning a big family trip, I first research the location; then I write detailed info on index cards about possible things to do, sites to visit, and places to dine. I include addresses, hours, pricing, and highlights. We then lay out all the cards on a table and choose our top picks. I bring one good guidebook that I leave at the hotel for reference. When we're out and about, all I carry are that day's cards, plus a few extras with backup ideas.

Lynn Anderson, Phoenix, Ariz.

THANKSGIVING TAKEAWAY We love to travel during Thanksgiving week. It's low season in some parts of the world, so it's cheaper and less crowded. Instead of turkey and football, my kids will always remember eating snake in Vietnam and warthog in Botswana!

Dave Schickling, Orange County, Calif.

FORWARD THINKING We show our preschoolers pictures of our destination, but we wait until a day or two before our departure; otherwise they'll get confused. On the day we actually travel, we explain the next three things we'll be doing: We will get in a car, go to an airport, and then get on the plane. Each time we knock an item off our list, we add another till we get to our destination. It makes the trip manageable and suspenseful.

F. P., New York, N.Y.

FAIRER FARES When booking flights online for your family, compare what it costs to purchase multiple tickets versus individual ones. If there aren't enough seats in one fare base, the group price sometimes defaults to the next-highest-priced ticket. When I searched for four tickets from Tulsa to Miami, each one was $309. Then I looked for individual tickets and found three for $279 and a fourth for $309. I saved $90!

David Bykowski, Broken Arrow, Okla.

DAY PLANNERS We like to divvy up vacation research among family members, allowing each person to schedule the events for a day however he or she wishes. It's a great way to get everyone involved in where we're going. We've found ourselves looking into everything from a city's best ice cream to how to rent paddleboats.

Catherine Murau, Ann Arbor, Mich.

TWO TRUMPS ONE<<<<<<<<<

Our teenage son is an only child, and
for many years we've let him invite
a friend along on our vacations.
It's more fun for him if he has a
companion, and that makes it easier
for us. His friend's family usually pays
for airfare and some of the pricier
excursions, while we cover food, lodging, and incidental costs.

Debby Schlesinger, Granada Hills, Calif.

EVENTS "R" US<<<<<<<<

Whatsonwhen.com covers more than 36,000 happenings and celebrations in 166 countries and lets you search by month, destination, or theme, so you can organize your trip according to your interests, whether blueberry festivals or children's theater.

Ray Alvarez, Anchorage, Alaska

YOUR OWN ACTION ADVENTURE! My son loved the 2004 movie *National Treasure*, so I organized a vacation around the sights shown in the film. One stop was the Lincoln Memorial in Washington, D.C. We also hit the National Zoo, the National Air and Space Museum, and Arlington National Cemetery. I've never seen a child happily take in so much history. Best of all, pretty much everything we did was free.

James Dodsworth, Jensen Beach, Fla.

GATHER YOUR FACTS Google Notebook, a service that allows users to clip information from many different Web sites and compile it all onto one Web page, is invaluable. I can log on from anywhere to view my Notebook and share my page with family and friends. A number of users have chosen to make their Notebooks public, which means you can search for, say, "Bay Area restaurants" and come up with a list of someone else's favorite spots.

Carli Entin, Hoboken, N.J.

16

The Smart Family's Passport

TEEN CHOICE AWARDS To make a California road trip exciting for our sons, who were 14 and 16 and big skateboarders, we had them research skate parks to visit along the way. More than 10 years later, it's a trip we're all still talking about. And, yes, we also got in visits to Venice Beach, Hearst Castle, and Alcatraz Island.

Pat Stewart, Maumee, Ohio

BRIGHT IDEA Print your itinerary details—including all confirmation numbers, telephone numbers, and the like—on colored paper. When you have to dig up specifics, it's easy to locate that piece of paper among other items you're carrying.

Beverly J. Rettus, Los Gatos, Calif.

SEE FOR YOURSELF To get a feel for a potential travel destination, I check out YouTube. Lots of people post videos from their trips, and you can get a real sense of what a town or beach looks like.

Rhonda Hingle, San Diego, Calif.

NOW THAT PRICE IS RIGHT I was booking tickets online for an upcoming flight to Europe from the East Coast. One particularly attractive fare was offered on a U.S. airline as well as on its foreign partner airline. Same plane, same flight, same base price. But it was more than $100 cheaper per ticket to book with the foreign airline versus the U.S. one. We saved more than $400 for four tickets!

Lori Uhl, Glenville, Pa.

POLITICAL ADVANTAGE If you're planning to spend time in Washington, D.C., always write in advance to your state's congressional representatives, requesting free maps, brochures, passes to attend sessions of Congress, and even discounted tour tickets.

J. Morrill, Alexandria, Va.

BARGAIN OF THE MINUTE If you want to find out where the U.S. dollar goes the furthest, go to the Office of Allowances page of the U.S. Department of State Web site (aoprals.state. gov). Click on the Foreign Per Diem Rates link. The site lists the maximum rates of hotels, meals, and incidentals in more than 1,000 locations around the world.

Barbara Zalot, Rocky Hill, Conn.

EARLY BIRDS We always try to book the first flight out in the morning because those planes often arrive at the airport the night before. You won't have to rely on an incoming plane, which could be delayed or canceled due to bad weather elsewhere.

George Glover, Brunswick, Maine

LOOK BOOKS I like the DK Eyewitness Travel Guides because they're filled with great pictures. Before we take a trip, I show them to my kids and have them highlight or flag the things they think we should see.

Jacki Barber, New London, N.H.

GIRL POWER<<<<<<<<

For $12 a year, anyone can join the Girl Scouts of the USA and receive access to the World Centers that the World Association of Girl Guides and Girl Scouts (wagggs.org) runs in Mexico, India, England, and Switzerland. I stayed at Pax Lodge in London for $79.

Alison L. Bentley, Poughkeepsie, N.Y.

RESERVATION INSPIRATION OpenTable (opentable.com) is a free service that lets you make restaurant reservations all over the United States. It has a points system that allows you to earn free meals. Most reservations are worth 100 points, but some are worth 1,000. If you choose those, it's easy to rack up 5,000 points, which entitles you to a $50 gift certificate to any of the site's restaurants.

Lisa Silverman, Valley Village, Calif.

PICTURE THIS Before a recent trip to Puerto Rico, I went to the photo-sharing site Flickr (flickr.com) and searched for images of the island. Just going through people's snapshots helped me decide what we wanted to do on our trip. And once we got there, it was fun to see familiar sites.

Debbie Morantes, San Antonio, Tex.

HOME-COURT ADVANTAGE If you're traveling to Great Britain, you can save a considerable amount on lodging by accessing the UK Web sites of hotel chains. For example, travelodge.co.uk has a section for offers and competitions, with rates starting at $27 per room.

Amy B. Cochran, Fort Edward, N.Y.

ON THE METRO BEAT When we're planning to visit a city that has a subway, I like to review the transit map in advance to familiarize myself with the system. Amadeus.net makes this easy—just click on Trip Tools to access the maps.

Alan Brill, Staten Island, N.Y.

DISCARDED DISCOUNTS You can save big by purchasing coupons and gift certificates on eBay. I've found great prices on airline and Amtrak tickets; car rentals; entrance to amusement parks such as SeaWorld, Disney, and Universal Studios; as well as overnights at many hotels. For example, I bought a $30 savings coupon for SeaWorld for only $1. Simply search for your destination and then type in "coupon" or "gift certificate."

Nathaniel V. Greenwood, Hummelstown, Pa.

GREAT EXPECTATIONS My family travels with a notebook in which we all write down the one thing we most want to do on our trip (it has to be an activity we can all participate in). At breakfast, we peruse our lists and plan our day. We carry the notebook and use it as a journal. It makes a rich, and often hilarious, record.

Cynthia Johnston, Omaha, Nebr.

02

ORGANIZING
ALL THAT GEAR:

THE KEY TO
PACKING

FAMILY BAGGAGE When our son and daughter were younger, we bought wheeled nylon duffel bags in a different color for each person. Having colors made it easy to do a last-minute check to confirm that everyone's bag was loaded into the car.

Angie Matkins, Monroe, La.

HANDS-ON APPROACH I found a fun way to identify our luggage at baggage claim. I bought red, blue, and yellow fabric paint from a crafts store and had my kids cover each bag with their handprints.

Kim Pilsbury, Woodstock, Ga.

READY TO WEAR Pack your children's (and your own!) complete outfits—shirt, shorts/pants, underwear, socks—in gallon-size reusable Ziploc bags. Each morning, instead of tearing apart the suitcase to find various items, all your child has to do is grab a bag.

Kim Thompson, Long Lake, Minn.

WALK THIS WAY Unless you're traveling with an infant who is too young to sit up, try to make do with only an umbrella stroller—one that folds up easily and compactly. Most airlines allow you to check it at the gate, and it'll be conveniently waiting right outside the plane door when you arrive.

Helene Honeybone, Dallas, Tex.

ATTACHED AT THE HIP<<<<<

I bought my sons fanny packs to use as toiletry bags. When they need to brush their teeth or comb their hair, they just grab their individual packs. This tip comes in especially handy when you're vacationing at a campground.

Debra Kushnick, Marietta, Ga.

MINE AND YOURS Distribute everyone's clothes throughout all the family's suitcases. If you're flying and a bag gets lost, at least everyone has some of their things. Plus, if you're on a road trip, you don't have to take out all the bags at every stop.

Jan Ecklund, Conneaut, Ohio

LIKE MOTHER, LIKE DAUGHTER I keep a master packing list on my computer for my daughter and me. Whenever we travel, I update the list and print a copy for my daughter. She feels very grown-up packing her own things, and I feel less pressured. On big trips, I bring the checklist to review and make sure we don't leave anything behind when we're heading home.

Laura Sueoka, submitted at BudgetTravel.com

FISHERMAN'S CATCHALL Rather than filling our bags with batteries, memory cards, asthma inhalers, and countless other small items, I now wear a fishing vest while on vacation. The vest has lots of small pockets to hold all the things we might need throughout the day, and it leaves my hands free. Better yet, at airport security, I don't have to empty my pockets. I just put the vest through the scanner, walk through the X-ray, and head to my gate.

Doug Broleman, St. Louis, Mo.

BLANKIE STATEMENTS Bring along a comfort item from home. Both of our kids are allowed one stuffed animal and one blanket; that seems to make the transition to new places much easier.

Laura Schaefer, Pittsburgh, Pa.

FLIP YOUR LID<<<<<<

If you're packing a container that has a
pump or a cap—such as the bottles that
hold lotion or sunscreen—replace the top
with one from a 20-ounce soda bottle.
It's almost always a perfect fit, and you
won't have to worry about leaks.

Emily Butler, Mechanicsburg, Pa.

A SORTED AFFAIR<<<<<<

I hate having to rummage through a
suitcase to find something, so I group
similar items in clear plastic bags—
all the socks in one bag, underwear
in another, and so on. It's like a filing
system for suitcases.

Diana Graves, Crested Butte, Colo.

A GIFT THAT KEEPS ON GIVING I have taken to turning those brightly colored plastic gift cards (once they're fully used up) into luggage ID tags. I stick a white label with my contact information on the back of each one, punch a hole at the end, and attach the card to my family's luggage. The vibrant designs make our suitcases stand out in a sea of look-alikes.

Philip Treu, St. Charles, Mo.

COUNT DOWN For kids old enough to read numbers, bring a stopwatch and a mechanical counter. It's amazing how many things can be timed and tallied. Lots of entertainment value for little added expense or weight.

Nadine MacLane, Seattle, Wash.

CREATE STRUCTURE A large soft-sided piece of luggage with a pull-up handle has an uneven inside, making it hard to pack. If you put shoes and other odd-shaped items in the bottom and then cut a piece of cardboard to fit the luggage and place it on top, you'll have an even surface on which to place pants, shirts, and so on.

Monica McCord, Easton, Pa.

NO THERMOS NECESSARY After looking for years for the perfect toiletries bag, I finally discovered one that is just right: a soft-sided lunch box purchased at the supermarket. It has an outer zipped pocket with compartments and slots perfect for often-used items like toothbrushes and toothpaste. There's a removable zipper pouch inside (meant for an ice pack) that nicely accommodates smaller, hard-to-find items like nail files and pill bottles. The remaining space is just right for larger items like shampoo and hand lotion. Other helpful features include a small handle, a shoulder strap, and a waterproof easy-to-clean interior. As an elementary school teacher, I know firsthand that it'll last: It was designed to withstand daily use by kids!

Jennifer Minton, Glencoe, Calif.

CORK IT If you're bringing scissors in your luggage, stick the points into a cork. That way you can be sure your kids won't accidentally cut themselves while rooting through a bag.

Dolores Calamari, Hilton Head Island, S.C.

PARKA PILLOW While packing for a camping trip to Yellowstone National Park, it occurred to me that, instead of taking pillows, we could place our down coats inside our pillowcases. Just turn each coat inside out, form it into a pillow shape, and stuff it in the case.

Kathy Walle, Gettysburg, Pa.

Q-TIP TIP M&M's Minis tubes work great for carrying Q-tips. They're the perfect length and easy to find in a toiletry bag—though once spotted, they'll inevitably disappoint your kids.

Julie Schell, Ellison Bay, Wis.

SEND 'EM PACKING My sons have been in charge of their own carry-on bags—containing not only teddy bears and games, but underwear and toiletries—since they were 3 years old. Before we take a trip, I give them a calendar marked with the days we'll be away, so they can figure out what they'll need. This gets them excited about the vacation and teaches them to be responsible and independent.

Maria Aubry, Setauket, N.Y.

36

The Smart Family's Passport

A BRIGHT ID Many pet stores have machines that engrave a small metal disk with your pet's name and your contact info. These disks can also serve as ID tags for luggage. If the airline loses a suitcase and the outside tag is missing, your contact information will still be available.

Kathleen Howe, Carrollton, Tex.

IN A JIF Always carry peanut butter. It comes in an easy-to-pack plastic jar, doesn't need refrigeration, is a great source of protein, and, when paired with bread, makes a quick, cheap meal. (Just don't forget to pack a plastic knife for spreading.)

Nancy Norman, Lancaster, N.Y.

THE BRUSH-OFF <<<<<<<<<<<

When packing skis in a travel bag,
I always include a combination
long-handled brush and ice scraper.
Rental cars in the mountains tend
to come with a handheld ice scraper,
but it's not enough when you get
up in the morning and discover
a foot of snow all over your car.
While others are stuck clearing snow
away with their sleeves and gloves, I'm
already at the gondola.

Henry McCown, Austin, Tex.

WATER YOU WAITING FOR? We all know to adjust our thermostats before a vacation, but did you ever think about your water heater? Right before my last trip, I looked at my heater and was surprised to find a "vacation" setting. It keeps the water warm but not as hot as you'd need to run the washing machine or take a shower.

Ceil Schlosser, Cincinnati, Ohio

PLAY YOUR CARDS RIGHT I keep our rewards and club cards in a small six-ring binder (about the size of a day planner) filled with plastic business-card-holder sheets I bought at an office-supply store. It's compact enough to stash in the glove compartment and means we don't have to fumble through our wallets.

Erika Jones-Haskins, Chesterfield, Va.

THE DIAPER-BAG DAYPACK Even if your kids are toilet trained, I've found that a diaper bag is great to carry on vacation. In Bermuda, the waterproof interior kept our passports, credit cards, tour books, extra clothes, and beach towels dry while we were near the water. The insulated bottle carrier kept one drink cold. The separate pouch, usually used for soiled baby clothes, held our wet swimsuits. There were pouches and elastic bands for sunscreen, sunglasses, and a camera. And the latest styles don't even look like diaper bags.

Susan Rixman, Louisville, Ky.

SNACK-SIZE GOO If you'd rather not buy travel-sized versions of your favorite products, use Ziploc bags to portion out a small quantity. The bag can even act as an applicator: Just snip a corner and squeeze out the contents.

Richard Czarnecki, Wayne, N.J.

STUFF IT! Our soft-sided travel bag loses its shape unless it's fully packed. To fill interior gaps, I use those inflated plastic pouches commonly sent as buffers with mail-order goods. I also put an air pouch or two in exterior zip pockets and toss them later, when we have dirty laundry to stuff in those pockets instead.

Robert Behr, Williamstown, Mass.

WATER MUSIC We take a shower radio when traveling to the beach. They're small enough to pack in almost any bag, they hold up great in wet locations, and, because they're pretty cheap (usually under $15), we don't beat ourselves up if we accidentally forget them.

Casey O'Connell, Warren, Mich.

A WINNING FORMULA In addition to serving its intended function, a neoprene wine-bottle carrier can protect a breakable souvenir and keep a bottle of water or a baby bottle cool.

Wendy VanHatten, Sergeant Bluff, Iowa

CASE CLOSED! Glue a business card inside all your family's eyeglass cases. I do this and have had lost glasses returned several times.

Lou Stover, Cardiff, Calif.

FILLED WITH PILLS I've found that empty dental-floss containers make great travel pillboxes. When you remove the little spool inside, there's room for a few vitamins or several smaller pills.

Helene Bayona, High Point, N.C.

POUCH POWER Those drawstring fabric bags that sheet sets come in are great for packing. I use them to keep my kids' dirty shoes away from clothes. And the large bag my comforter came in is perfect for beach trips. I tote towels, lotion, and toys in it.

Debbie Simorte, Platte City, Mo.

PB AND JEWELRY When staying in hotel rooms I used to put my jewelry in clean ashtrays, which are now mostly a thing of the past. Instead, I bring a cleaned out plastic lid from a peanut butter jar. It's the perfect size for my jewelry, I can put it on a high shelf far from my kids' hands, and the bright color is easy to see, so I never leave it behind.

Joy Johnson, Stuart, Fla.

WEIGH TO GO! After spending two weeks in Alaska—one on land and one on a cruise—we had collected more souvenirs than we'd anticipated. Worried about overweight-luggage fees at the airport, we hauled our suitcases to the cruise ship's gym and weighed them on one of the scales. We kept rearranging the contents until each family member's bag weighed less than 50 pounds (but barely!).

Nancy Boehmer, Bridgeton, Mo.

OUT OF YOUR HAIR Slip a scrunchie or ponytail holder through the handles of your family's suitcase and pull one end through the other. The resulting loop is handy for holding an extra sweater or a teddy bear (just make sure it's secure!) as you make your way around the airport.

Leonore Bourgeault, Belmar, N.J.

KEEP YOUR COOLER My husband uses a small soft-sided cooler as his carry-on bag. When we arrive at our destination, we have a cooler to use in the hotel, in the rental car, or at the beach.

Mary Wohlers, Fairfax, Iowa

SACKS APPEAL Always throw a few empty Ziploc bags in various sizes into your suitcase. You'll end up using them constantly—for wet bathing suits or extra food, to protect your camera in the rain, even to wear over your head in a storm.

Joseph C. Bauer, Orange, Calif.

HANG ON—AND ON These days even the nicest hotels have a lack of hooks and towel bars in the bedroom and bathroom. With several wet towels and bathing suits to hang, I now know to always pack a stash of removable hooks. They're inexpensive, don't take up much room in a suitcase, and can be applied and removed without leaving marks. Then you can reuse them on your next trip.

Marilyn Opp, Stillwater, Minn.

SEALED WITH A BALLOON Last summer we went to see my mother-in-law, and she gave the kids a bag of balloons to play with. When it was time to head home, I decided to use the balloons to keep our toiletry containers sealed. I cut off the tips of the balloons, stretched them over the tops of small containers, and stretched the remaining halves over the larger containers' lids. Not one of the containers exploded.

Bibi Gefre, Stillwater, Minn.

THE FLYING STROLLER We recently took our kids to Walt Disney World, followed by a Disney cruise. We wanted to save money in the parks by bringing our own double stroller rather than renting one, but we needed a smaller stroller for the cruise. We found that our umbrella stroller fit perfectly in the bag that came with our camping chair. And because the stroller was enclosed, we were able to check it as luggage.

Angela MacKinnon, New Freedom, Pa.

EIGHT IS ENOUGH<<<<<<<<

When we're away for more than
one week, I always pack eight days'
worth of clothes. That way, I don't do
any laundry until I've really had
a vacation.

Lorraine Hughes, submitted at
BudgetTravel.com

CHAPTER THREE

BORN TO TRAVEL:

VACATIONING with BABIES

BUDGET

TRAVEL

[✈ ✈ ✈]

03

<BT<<<<<<<<<<<<<<<<<<<<<<<<<<<<<<
9781594744488<<<<<<<<<<<<<<<<<10

THE SILENT TREATMENT Whenever you're flying with a baby, bring along a few extra pairs of disposable earplugs to give to passengers sitting nearby. If your baby cries, they can continue their flight in peace. You may not be able to control your infant, but at least you can show that you care about your neighbors' eardrums!

Heather NeRoy, Hemet, Calif.

MAKES DIAPERING A PICNIC Plastic tablecloths are excellent changing-table covers. Cut one into pieces about three square feet each. They take up almost no space in a diaper bag and are a lifesaver when you're forced to change your baby or squirmy toddler in a public restroom. Just toss the squares when you're finished.

Carol McNulty, Mechanicsburg, Pa.

ROOM TO ROAM I'm a new mom and have already discovered one thing: When traveling with a very young child, get a one-bedroom suite, not just a room. Extra space and a nice patio or view will help you avoid that "trapped by the sleeping baby" feeling. A kitchenette is invaluable for cleaning bottles, storing and warming milk, and stocking your own snacks.

Jennifer Garske, Washington, D.C.

BREAST IDEA EVER! When my husband and I took a train trip through Switzerland with our two sons, the youngest was only 4 months old and still nursing. Packing light was a priority, but I insisted on including my bulky breast-feeding pillow (much to my husband's chagrin). We stuffed the pillow's cover with burp cloths and changes of clothes for the kids. I was able to feed the baby in comfort, and all the items I needed were close at hand.

Kari Schilling, Bamberg, Germany

SPACE IT OUT With a baby, it's all about staying at vacation rentals or time-shares. When your baby cries or the whole family is up at dawn, you don't have to worry about bothering others. Best of all, you don't have to go out to eat for every meal.

Nadine MacLane, Seattle, Wash.

AIR REPORT Flyingwithkids.com has everything you need to know about planning a flight with infants and children, including information on gear and packing, not to mention tips on what to expect at airports.

Peggy Bennett, West Hartford, Conn.

MACGYVER-APPROVED I always pack a roll of duct tape. In addition to being handy as a family-luggage identifier (put a colorful strip on the outside of everyone's bags), it's perfect for baby-proofing a hotel room. I use it to tie up loose curtain and electrical cords, patch sharp corners, keep drawers closed, and cover outlets.

Pamm McFadden, Boulder, Colo.

NIGHT CRAWLERS For long flights with an infant or 1-year-old, take the red-eye—the baby will sleep and won't get off schedule.

Jane Gillespie, Honolulu, Hawaii

LOOK, MA, NO HANDS! <<<<<

When traveling with infants, you have to stop several times a day to feed them. That's not always easy when you're also trying to catch a train or get to an event. We discovered Podee Baby Bottles, which were designed for parents with multiples. The nipple is attached to the bottle by a long, clear tube, so the baby sucks on it like a pacifier—no hands required. That allows us to give our girls their bottles while we drive or push them in the stroller.

Melissa Bowlen-Macomber, Edgewood, Md.

CHANGING TIMES Before booking a flight, find out if the plane has diaper-changing tables—many don't. In a pinch, you can always use your seat with a cover placed over it. But to avoid the hassle—and the dirty looks from seatmates—change your baby's diaper just before you board.

Felicity Nitz, Bronx, N.Y.

CRIB NOTES For a trip through Europe with our toddler, my husband and I bought KidCo's PeaPod travel bed—basically a small pop-up tent with a tiny inflatable mattress. It's much more compact than a travel crib (it even fits in our backpack). Everywhere we went, our daughter had the same bed, so she was comfortable with her surroundings and fell asleep easily.

Peggy Sue Loroz, Cheney, Wash.

WHO'S ON FIRST? When taking a baby or small child on an international flight, instead of booking three seats in the same row, opt for two adjacent seats plus a single in the next row back. That way only one person is "on duty" at a time.

Nadine MacLane, Seattle, Wash.

SWEET RELIEF I give my toddler a lollipop before takeoff and descent. The treat keeps her occupied, and all the swallowing helps prevent pressure from building up in her ears. Landings can be bumpy, so before you touch down, take the candy away—just to be on the safe side.

Joanna Ghosh, Boothwyn, Pa.

THINK NONSTOP<<<<<<<<<<

En route to St. Lucia, we realized that it just doesn't make sense to take a baby or toddler on a multileg journey: It's too exhausting for them and for you. We now set our sights on places that are reachable by direct flight. And when that's impossible, we break up the trip by spending a night somewhere along the way.

Margaret Lazer, Marietta, Ohio

Y HAUL? When my husband and I first traveled with our children, our luggage was weighed down by diapers, formula, and other necessities. To save space and hassle, we now buy most of these items on arrival. We also came across a Web site called babiestravellite.com, where we can order supplies and have them shipped anywhere in the world. And babysaway.com, a rental service with more than 70 locations across the United States, offers cribs, strollers, high chairs, and car seats.

Mina Camera, San Gabriel, Calif.

BOOK A BASSINET The greatest invention in the history of family travel is the flying bassinet, an amenity some European and Asian airlines offer free of charge to travelers with a baby. (Hint: You have to be seated in the bulkhead and it's best to request in advance.) We discovered it on an Air France flight from San Francisco to Paris when a flight attendant walked by, admired our 14-month-old daughter, and then reappeared with another attendant to snap a canvas cot onto the wall in front of us. Securely inside, our baby could sit up and happily gaze out at the world. She also snoozed while my husband and I ate dinner uninterrupted for the first time in 14 months.

Andrea Gemmet, San Francisco Peninsula, Calif.

RUBBER DUCKY NOT INCLUDED It can be difficult for parents to find a place to bathe an infant while on vacation. Showers obviously won't work, and the miniscule sinks generally found in hotel bathrooms aren't appropriate either. On our last cruise, we eliminated the problem by packing a small, inexpensive inflatable bathtub. (Ours cost only $8.) When we arrived, we blew it up and placed it in the bottom of the shower for an instant—and safe—baby bath.

Maria Diekema-Zuidema, Lewisville, N.C.

BABY'S FIRST MILES You're never too young to be a frequent flier. Register your kids with the airline's loyalty program when you pay for their first airfare. But note that many mileage programs will erase your miles if the account is inactive for 18 months; before that happens, donate the miles to a charity at miledonor.com.

Laura Hunt, Chicago, Ill.

SITTER SAVVY <<<<<<<<<<<

Wherever we go, we always try to locate a reputable babysitting agency. It gives us a much-needed break and also lets our child play with someone new.

Laura Schaefer, Pittsburgh, Pa.

CHAPTER FOUR

BUDGET TRAVEL

THE DRIVE:

ROAD-TRIP

TACTICS

(04)

USE YOUR HEAD! When you have a family of six and you're on a road trip, snacks are crucial. On one trip, we ran out of munchies. All that was left was a head of lettuce, so I broke off large handfuls and passed them out. To our surprise, the kids loved crunching on them! It's a new way to get some veggies into everyone, it doesn't make as much of a mess as chips, and it doesn't leave us thirsty. Ever since that trip, the kids double-check that I remember to bring some crunchy greens.

Sandra Beagley, Shawnigan Lake, B.C.

PLAYING FAVORITES Knowing that this year's family vacation included a 10-hour car ride (each way!), we decided to burn our own road-trip music CD. Each family member chose a few favorite songs, which we purchased and downloaded from the Internet. Now, whenever we hear one of the songs on the radio, it takes us right back to that particular vacation.

Bryan Holmes, Danville, Pa.

KEEP 'EM OCCUPIED Prior to a long ride, visit your local dollar store and stock up on gifts for your kids. Wrap each item; then, to keep the kids busy, dole them out at designated points (every 50 miles, or hour, or when you pass a certain landmark). Quiet gifts are best: washable markers and coloring books, finger puppets, toy dinosaurs, and travel games that don't have small pieces.

Eva K. Chamberlain, Chula Vista, Calif.

MEALS ON WHEELS Pack a cooler with sandwich fillings, bread, fruit, snacks, and drinks. Then brake at rest stops to enjoy your meals. It's cheaper than dining in restaurants, and most rest stops have grassy areas where kids can run around and stretch their legs.

Lauren Williams, Columbia, Mo.

NOW HEAR THIS! At Cracker Barrel restaurants, you can rent and return audiobooks at any location, which is great for road trips. If you finish a book during your journey, it's possible to return it at another location and pick up a new one. You pay for the first book (from $10) and, when it's returned, check out another at a reduced fee.

Harriet Diamond, Boynton Beach, Fla.

WITHIN REACH Hang a shoe organizer on the back of the passenger seat and insert kids' stuffed animals, books, and games in the pockets. Having everything close at hand has proven to prevent meltdowns along the way.

Jennifer Casasanto, Newton, Mass.

ROUTE FOR THE HOME TEAM<<<<

Every summer, we drive out West
from Pennsylvania with our two kids.
To avoid that infamous road trip question ("Are we there yet?"),
I give each child a map with our
route highlighted. Along the way, they
can match up the town names with
the road signs we pass. They always
know exactly where we are and how
much farther we have to
go until we get there.

Machell McCoy, Carlisle, Pa.

CRACK THE CODE If you Google "rental-car discount codes," you'll find a number of Web sites offering consolidated lists of these codes. You just may discover you're eligible for a load of reductions.

Lawrence Spinetta, Poquoson, Va.

BIN THERE, DONE THAT When my grandchildren turn 12 years old, I take each one on a summer drive. The trips range from two weeks to a month and require careful packing. I've learned to put our clothes and snacks in plastic bins that fit in the back of my minivan. We each bring a small bag and pack it every evening with items we'll need for that night and the next day: no lugging heavy suitcases in and out of hotels.

Patsy Maddox, Fairfax, Va.

IT'S ELEMENTARY After you've been cooped up in a car, scenic overlooks and rest stops aren't nearly as fun for kids as playgrounds are. And an hour of burning up energy dashing between swings and slide will gain you at least an hour of more adult-friendly activities.

Chris Bruns, submitted at BudgetTravel.com

LEAVE THE MONSTERS BEHIND We have a big, heavy Britax car seat that we use when we're home. But after hefting it on plane trips for use in our rental car, we bought a well-rated, inexpensive, lightweight one to use as a travel seat. The spare also comes in handy when we're riding in someone else's car.

Laura Hunt, Chicago, Ill.

PLAY AS YOU GO<<<<<<<<<<<

Old-fashioned games, like counting
license plates, 20 Questions, and
Name That Tune, are fun for everyone.
Visit the Web site momsminivan.com
for a list of car activities as well as
song lyrics that you can print out
for sing-alongs.

J. Lipkin, Aspen, Colo.

COUNTER INTUITIVE<<<<<<

When you're exploring the United States, deli counters in grocery stores are great mealtime alternatives to restaurants and fast-food fare. The food is fresh, there's a good variety (hot and cold), and economically it's a great break. I've bought a complete hot meal, including beverage, for $3 from a local deli.

Teresa G. Barcus, St. Paul, Minn.

OUR OWN ODYSSEY Before a long journey, I attached games and puzzles (found online for free) to clipboards and stuck them in our car's seat-back pockets for each of my children. I also made up pages labeled with the states we'd visit and listed facts about each, including landmarks to watch for. I folded the pages and sealed them with stickers, marking them "Open in Virginia," "Open in New York," and so on. Our kids had something new—and educational—to do in each state.

Deb Baker, Americus, Ga.

SIGN WATCHERS On a family RV trip across 12 states, I took a picture of the "Now Leaving" sign whenever we left one state and the "Welcome to" sign for the next state we entered. It proved to be a simple way to keep our photos organized—and it kept our kids busy looking for the signs.

Lori Lenton, Red Deer, Alberta

GOODIE AND PLENTY <<<<<<

Before taking my granddaughter on a road trip to Disneyland, I made goodie bags for her. On the outside was a picture—a bridge I knew we'd be passing, for example; inside was something that she could do in the car. She got to open the surprise package when we came across whatever was drawn on the bag. I also had bags for treats in the motel room.

Mary Jarvis, Puyallup, Wash.

DRIVE-IN THEATER<<<<<<

If you have a DVD player in your car,
sign up with Redbox (redbox.com).
You can rent and return movies
at more than 14,000 locations
around the country, including many
McDonald's and Wal-Mart stores. This
way, you don't have to bother packing
loads of DVDs for your
trip, and you'll have new movies
to watch along the way.

Becky Welton, St. Louis, Mo.

EAT AND RUN If you're lucky enough to find a fast-food restaurant with a playground, let your kids run around and play while you eat. Get their food to go and have them eat in the car. No one will feel rushed.

Heather M. Hickox, Fairhope, Ala.

LAUGHING ALL THE WAY Some of our fondest memories of road trips with our sons involve Mad Libs. You can buy these inexpensive fill-in-the-blank books, or get creative and make your own. Designate a reader/recorder, and the rest of the family comes up with the missing verbs, nouns, and adjectives. The results are hilarious. Try using popular songs or nursery rhymes ("Three Blind Mice" turned into "Sixteen Bumpy Squirrels" on one trip). A dreary ride will become a car full of giggles.

Eva K. Chamberlain, Chula Vista, Calif.

MOVIE TIME When our grandkids asked how long our drive would take, we told them "two movies" (or about four hours). They loved that reply and didn't have to keep asking us how much longer we had to go. Now we always give them driving times in DVDs.

Cyndy Nordyke, Hurst, Tex.

ORDER IN THE BACKSEAT Car clutter can really take over a 10-day road trip. To prevent it, I give each of my kids a plastic six-quart container with a lid and tell them that everything they want during the trip has to go in the box and stay there when not in use. This way, they're each responsible for keeping their own games, books, and souvenirs in order.

Tracey A. Presslor, Joplin, Mo.

SPLASH LANDING Early starts are essential on road trips. The children sleep in the car for the first hour or two, and then we stop for a wake-up breakfast. We always try to hit a park at lunchtime to let the kids run off some steam. This way we can finish our day's driving early enough to go for a swim at a motel.

Lila Held, Garden Grove, Calif.

DOG'S BEST FRIEND Bring a Frisbee when you travel. It's fun for your kids and your dog, and it can double as your pet's food or water bowl at pit stops.

Wendy Mathia, Silver Spring, Md.

ROAD FOOD FIX<<<<<<<<<<

I clip restaurant-chain coupons and
store them in the glove compartment.
On car trips, when my family and
I eat most of our meals on the road,
we enjoy the discounts.

Rebecca Ayala, Houston, Tex.

HOP STOP A jump rope for each of kid can come in handy. At a rest stop, they can hop their little hearts out. Back in the car, they won't be as antsy and may even sleep a little bit.

Simon Mulverhill, San Antonio, Tex.

BIG-BOX WHEELS When booking a car rental, check out costco.com. It generally offers cheaper rates than the sites of major rental companies, and Alamo and National waive the additional-driver fee for Costco members.

Junji Takeshita, Honolulu, Hawaii

SAVE YOUR RESOURCES To make the most of my mobile bag of tricks, I devised an "Only One Thing at a Time" method. It works this way: If my kids are watching a movie, they are not also eating a snack. And if they're enjoying a snack, they're not coloring as well. Using up multiple activities in a single time slot is the equivalent of starting out too fast in a marathon.

Heather M. Hickox, Fairhope, Ala.

COLLECTION AGENT Those insulated-foam can holders make great storage places in the car. They hold crayons and art supplies, glasses, receipts, and any other little thing that might get lost somewhere else.

Susan Hutchinson, Canton, Ohio

TAX RELIEF When you rent a car at an airport, you often have to pay extra taxes and fees. Instead, rent from a location away from the airport and have the rental company pick you up (many offer this service for free). We once saved more than $50.

Diane Ketcham, Naples, Fla.

FULLY LOADED On long drives, we always bring a cooler packed with cheese and crackers, yogurt, bottled water, grapes, apples, and whatever else our family likes that is reasonably healthy. Also essential: a roll of paper towels, Kleenex, paper cups, plastic silverware, ibuprofen, and a little travel knife. I even keep a file box in the car filled with brochures and trip info.

Jacki Barber, New London, N.H.

PUMP PERKS Get a credit card from a company with gas stations nationwide. Many offer a percentage rebate, a gift card, or a certain percent off for an introductory period. For example, the BP card offers a 5 percent rebate on BP purchases up to $500: when you've accrued $25 in rebates, you can choose a gift card, a check, or a donation to The Conservation Fund. You also get a 2 percent rebate on travel- and dining-related expenditures, and a 1 percent rebate on all other purchases.

Amy Sutton, Farmdale, Ohio

BARGAIN CAR INSURANCE I apply vinyl bumper stickers—the kind that peel off without leaving a mark—onto our rental cars. With the car dressed up like it's a local, we don't have to worry about thieves who target tourists.

Chris Manos, Centennial, Colo.

CHAPTER FIVE

AIRPORTS AND AIRPLANES:

FLYING WITH THE YOUNG AND RESTLESS

CH - - - - - - - - - - - - 5

IMMIGRATION 20YCBB

Flying with the Young and Restless

WAIT AT THE GATE The early-boarding opportunities airlines offer to travelers with young children are great, but they can add as much as 30 minutes of confined time for our toddler. Now my husband boards at first call with all our carry-ons, and my daughter and I play in the waiting area until final call. By the time she and I get to our seats, my husband has them set up with snacks, juice cups, and coloring books. My daughter and I just buckle in.

Amanda Pekrul, Charlotte, N.C.

OR NOT... We tend to get on the plane first. It's less hassle to board an empty plane, and honestly if you wait until last call, those few extra minutes at the gate don't add up to much.

Jody Halsted, Ankeny, Iowa

THE FLYING TENT For quiet time when plane-bound, clip one end of an airline blanket into the fold-up tray and the other under the headrest (behind the child). Voilà: a "tent" that lets your toddler nap better on the plane. We put this together one night while stuck on a runway for almost six hours, and it saved the day. My son rarely naps anymore but still asks for an airplane tent, if only for playtime.

Roy Youngblood, Chicago, Ill.

MOVING PICTURES We have our kids pick out DVDs ahead of time. On board, we give them good headsets so that everyone else isn't subjected to the fluctuating volume. And we try never to forget the eight-hour battery!

Michael and Aviva Black, Oakland, Calif.

DISTRACTING ACT<<<<<<<<

By age 3 or 4, most kids are ready to carry their own small travel backpack. Fill it with surprise treats to occupy downtime—layovers, long flights, hotel stays—as well as a few familiar items from home. For older kids, include a notebook and encourage them to keep a travel diary.

Joan White, Dallas, Tex.

SEPARATE BUT EQUAL Assign one parent the essentials (diapers, wipes, snacks), and let the other carry the fun stuff (crayons, toys, books). You'll know which bag to scrounge through for the playing cards or the animal crackers.

F. P., New York, N.Y.

HELLO, CAPTAIN I'm a pilot for Virgin America and I think it's great when kids want to visit the cockpit. When the plane's on the ground with the jet bridge attached, we do allow visitors (at the captain's discretion). I remember how interested I was as a child going to the airport. Consider making a logbook for your kids so that pilots can write in your flight time and sign it.

Edward Yanock, Phoenix, Ariz.

LUG IT OR LEAVE IT The FAA recommends that children be secured in car seats. Unfortunately, the seats aren't made to fit in airplanes, and carrying them through the narrow aisles, not to mention fastening them in, is tricky. And most kids have their legs crammed against the seat in front, all but ensuring they'll kick it. The good news is that there is an FAA-approved alternative: a safety harness for kids weighing 22–44 pounds (available for $75 at kidsflysafe.com).

Laura Hunt, Chicago, Ill.

DIVIDE AND CONQUER We book two window seats and two middle seats for us and our two boys, thus avoiding countless fights and tantrums by giving each child his own window. Plus we each manage only one child. We try to secure seats in consecutive rows so that we can communicate easily and share toys and snacks. This might seem obvious, but it took a few rocky flights to figure it all out.

J. Wilson, Denver, Colo.

THE APPLE OF MY EAR<<<<<<

To avoid ear pain during flights, bring along an apple. When you feel the plane begin to descend—about 25 minutes before arrival—start snacking. The chewing and swallowing will keep ears in good shape. I'm a pilot, and it works every time!

Capt. Mike Filippell, Tower Lakes, Ill.

EARLY-BIRD SPECIAL When my wife and I fly with our young children, one of us preorders a special meal (kosher, gluten-free, etc.). These are almost always served at the beginning of the meal service, so one adult can eat while the other watches the children. When the rest of the meals are served, whoever has already eaten goes on kid duty.

Scott Barber, Harpenden, U.K.

LACE LOGIC Even children are required to remove their shoes at airport security. To simplify the experience, have your family travel in slip-ons.

Troy Dangerfield, San Francisco, Calif.

FULL DISCLOSURE Years ago, an airline rearranged our seats, leaving our two young grandsons seated rows away. Recently, an airline agent told me that when making reservations involving children, you should always mention their ages. If the airline ends up needing to reassign seats, gate agents will take the ages into consideration and try to keep the kids near a related adult.

Dianne Winney, Edwardsville, Ill.

UFOS As a flight attendant, I'm always amazed by the stuff people leave behind. Most of it never gets back to its rightful owner because there's no way of knowing who the owner is. To avoid misplacing your property, put things into your carry-on after using them—never on the floor or in the seat-back pocket. Label important items like books or games with return-address labels so that airlines can contact you when your belongings are found.

Doug Hummell, Houston, Tex.

EASY SEAT<<<<<<<<<<<<<<<

I used to check my toddler's car seat on flights, but now that many airlines charge for extra luggage, I keep it with me. Because the seat is so heavy and bulky, I bought a Tote-a-Tot (toteatot.com, $30), a strap that attaches the seat to any small roller suitcase. That way I don't have to carry it. Best of all, when I board I can check the seat at the door for free.

Cinzia Cervato, Ames, Iowa

PREP YOUR CREW When our daughter Ella was 2 and very attached to her stuffed Elmo and her blankie, we were concerned about her reaction on an upcoming plane trip, when she would have to be separated from them at security. Weeks before, my husband repeatedly described to Ella what to expect, painting it like a grand adventure. Once at the airport, Ella voluntarily put Elmo and the blankie on the belt so they could go for their ride and get their picture taken.

Lauren Williams, Columbia, Mo.

IN PLANE SIGHT Before plane trips, I download TV shows onto an iPod. To view hands-free, put a plastic airline cup on your tray table and place the iPod inside. The screen will be just above the lip—the perfect viewing position.

Kristi Wright, Norman, Okla.

PLAYOVER If you find yourself at Chicago O'Hare with a lengthy layover, consider going to the airport Hilton. A day-use fee of $15 allows you access to the hotel's swimming pool and gym.

Erin Caslavka, Carlsbad, Calif.

MOM-SENSE We always bring lots of snacks and sandwiches to have treats at the ready. The food goes in our carry-ons along with an extra set of clothes for the kids, medications, and (if we're heading to a beach) bathing suits. Even if our checked bags are delayed, our vacation begins on arrival.

Michael and Aviva Black, Oakland, Calif.

MUSIC IN THE AIR Now that airlines charge for everything, it's a good idea to save old headphones for use on future flights. When my daughter flew cross-country, I gave my headphones to her 3- and 5-year-old children. They loved punching the buttons and listening to the music.

Anne Zumstein, Marblehead, Mass.

GROUND CONTROL Before a recent trip, I learned we were going to have a four-hour layover in Detroit around dinnertime. Through an online search I found metroairport.com, a site that lists the Detroit airport's restaurants, shops, and ATMs by terminal and notes which concourse they're in. Many other airports have similar sites that are worth checking.

Heather Doherty, Lake Ariel, Pa.

PULLING YOUR WEIGHT By age 4, my kids could wheel their own small bags through the airport, and they enjoyed the responsibility. When they learned to read at age 5, I handed them packing lists. They quickly got the hang of choosing their clothes and checking the items off the list.

Sarah James, Exeter, N.H.

BOOK MOBILE Before my last long flight, I went to librivox. org and chose a bunch of books, short stories, and poems to download to my iPod—for free. The site has both adult and children's books, and the list is growing. All the titles are in the public domain, so there's no question of copyright infringement, and they're read by volunteers. You can also download them to your computer and burn them onto a CD.

Diane Bowman, Huntington Beach, Calif.

WEIGHT WATCHERS<<<<<<<<

When buying a ticket on an airline
you're unfamiliar with, ask about weight
limits for baggage and the charges for
excessive weight. We learned the hard
way that you need to pack lightly if
island-hopping in French Polynesia. The
airline even weighed our carry-ons.

Terry Lynn, East Atlantic Beach, N.Y.

LIFESAVERS I'm a flight attendant, and my route includes several mountain towns. The flights can get bumpy, so I carry a tin of strong peppermints with me and hand them out to passengers who are looking a little green at the gills. Peppermint oil, which is found in strong mints like Altoids, is one of Mother Nature's best cures for an upset tummy.

S. Reiser, Aurora, Colo.

GIVE 'EM THE RUNAROUND Before getting on a plane, rather than making your children wait quietly, allow them to run around like crazy in an empty corridor or waiting area. After a good romp, everyone will be ready for a rest during the flight.

F. P., New York, N.Y.

CHAPTER SIX

HOME AWAY FROM HOME: 6

YOUR LODGINGS

REST EASY Sleeping in strange hotel rooms can be unsettling for young kids. Buy your child a pillowcase with a favorite character—such as Scooby-Doo or Elmo—and use it at home as well as on vacation. It will help make a hotel room that much more familiar.

Heather Crow, Rio Rancho, N.Mex.

TOWEL I.D. When traveling with a group, we always bring along several clothespins, which we write our names on with permanent marker and clip to our towels. It makes for easy identification, and we never have to wonder who used which towel.

Linette Holliday, Bakersfield, Calif.

TIMELY GIFTS Before traveling with young kids, buy a present—something quiet—for each one. Then when you arrive at your hotel, sit the kids down and tell them you're giving them a "hotel gift." While they play with their new toys, you'll be able to unpack in peace. Plus they'll have a souvenir, so you won't have to purchase something you know they won't use.

Debbie Roche, Winterville, N.C.

LITTLE BOY'S ROOM When my husband and I first stayed in hotels with our 2-year-old, he'd wake up at all hours and think it was time to play. We now pack a pop-up tent and set it up in a corner with books, a blanket, and a few small stuffed animals. The tent folds down to a 14-inch circle and weighs about a pound. My son has his own "room" when we vacation, and we all get to sleep through the night!

Geri Kronyak, Boonton, N.J.

DIY ROOM SERVICE My mom and I were exhausted after a long day of sightseeing in New York City. Our hotel offered free Wi-Fi and I had my laptop with me, so instead of trekking out again for dinner, I went to menupages.com and looked up the menus of nearby restaurants. You can search the site by neighborhood and sort by restaurants that will deliver—so handy when you have kids in tow!

Jessica Bishop, Tuscaloosa, Ala.

DOOR PRIZE The magnets you use on a refrigerator will also stick well to the inside of most hotel- and motel-room doors, transforming them into makeshift bulletin boards. Post theater tickets, itineraries, reminder notes, and any other useful information; then grab what you need before leaving the room for the day.

Karen Hartz, Millersville, Md.

JUST ADD WATER Whenever we stay at a hotel whose rate doesn't include a continental breakfast, I bring several packages of instant oatmeal. Even rooms without a microwave often have a coffeemaker, so heating water isn't a problem. We all make our own oatmeal in the coffee cups provided (spoons are usually available, too, but I bring plastic ones just in case). The meal is done quickly, and we can get an earlier jump on the day.

Julie Bunczak, Wausau, Wis.

CHEZ VACATION For us, the ideal way to take a family vacation is to rent a house or condo. We've done it several times in Maine as well as in England. Cost-wise it works out to be less than a hotel, and you get space to run around, plus a kitchen, so you can have breakfast in your pajamas and actually relax.

Sara A. Ward, Fairfax, Va.

RESORT TO IT<<<<<<<<<<<<<

Even if you're staying at a standard resort hotel, take advantage of the day passes sold by many all-inclusive resorts. The passes—which give visitors access to the facilities, such as restaurants, swimming pools, and beach chairs—are primarily designed for cruise passengers on day trips, but anyone can obtain them for about $50 for adults and $25 for kids.

Mandy Vieregg, Waco, Tex.

WHATEVER FLOATS YOUR BOAT During a family trip to the beach last summer, our hotel room was one bed short. My daughter threw her inflatable beach raft on the floor and said, "I can sleep on this!" We found extra sheets, blankets, and a pillow in the closet and fixed up a bed for her. Since then, the raft has gone along with her on sleepovers and camping trips.

Amy Vega, Cameron, N.C.

READY, SET, GLOW Finding the bathroom in the middle of the night in a strange hotel room or cruise-ship cabin can be a challenge. Leaving the bathroom light on seems wasteful and makes the room too bright for sleeping. We used to travel with a night-light but couldn't always find a convenient place to plug it in. We've recently discovered a better solution: plastic light sticks. They come in several glow-in-the-dark colors and are activated by bending the tube into a circle and connecting the ends. Each evening, we hook one of the loops over the bathroom-door handle, where it provides a gentle glow through the night.

Carol Attar, Grosse Pointe Woods, Mich.

GO CONFIGURE When traveling with a group, it can be tough to figure out hotel-room arrangements. Instead of choosing your room, ask the reservations clerk what he or she would recommend as the best deal for your situation. We're a family of six, and I always tell the agent the kids' ages and who can share a bed. We've been given great solutions, such as two double rooms with roll-aways, and a family room for five with a roll-away.

Catherine Douglass, Tacoma, Wash.

VILLA VALUES To find a reasonably priced French villa or apartment to rent, try going directly to the owner through a site such as abritel.fr (click on the British flag for English). I arranged to spend two weeks in an apartment in Brittany and one week in an apartment in the Loire Valley, all for a total of $800.

Suzanne Maurice-Roberts, Staunton, Va.

NOT SO SWIMMINGLY<<<<<<<<<<

My family and I made reservations for a beach condo on Maui. Upon arrival, we were shocked to see a sign at the beach that read NO SWIMMING. We learned our lesson: make certain you specify a swimming beach when booking a vacation rental.

Ruth Herlean, Richmond, Va.

MINIBAR DAMAGE Your kids are less likely to whine for the overpriced snacks and candy in the minibar if you bring along a few of their favorite treats and slip them in among the off-limits goodies. (Just make sure the unit does not have a sensor.) For years our kids, now grown, marveled at how the places we stayed always seemed to know exactly what they liked!

Deborah Cloud, Fairfax, Va.

POP AND GO I always pack a bag or two of microwave popcorn. Most chains and many independent hotels have microwaves in either the guest rooms or a common area. The popcorn comes in especially handy when we arrive but aren't quite ready for dinner. I use the ice bucket as a bowl.

Stacey Maule, Eagle, Colo.

CLIMATE CONTROL Many hotels come equipped with heating/air-conditioning units that blow air with the velocity of a mini hurricane, often in the direction of the beds. We're sensitive to drafts, so I created a foldable cardboard air-deflector, about 6 inches by 30 inches, with tabs that fit into the unit's slots. It takes up little room in my suitcase and makes our stay much more comfortable.

Marge Picciano, Hamburg, N.Y.

THROW IN THE TOWEL We always bring our own towels to lay across our lounge chairs when we go to a beach resort, to a hotel with a pool, or on a cruise. Because most of the other guests use the white towels supplied by the resort, our chairs are easy to spot. We use the resort's towels to dry off if we go into the water.

Brian Metzler, Fair Lawn, N.J.

RATE CHASER Booking condos last minute can yield incredible bargains. ("Last minute" generally means a month or less before your stay.) Here's the best strategy: Buy your plane ticket and book a refundable hotel room you can use in case you can't find that bargain condo. Then, a month or so before your trip, start looking at last-minute sites—lastminutetravel.com, lastminute.com, and the like. If you find a deal, simply get a refund on the hotel room and pay the cancellation fee, if there is one. Using this technique, I found a great beachfront one-bedroom condo on Maui for $300 less than my first booking.

Joan Chyun, Irvine, Calif.

SKIRTING THE ISSUE Flight attendants often work vampire hours and have to sleep during the day. How do we keep the sunlight from leaking into our hotel rooms? We clip a skirt hanger (or two) to the middle of the drapes, sealing them together. This trick works equally great for parents trying to keep the light from waking up their children.

Elisabeth Joyce, San Clemente, Calif.

READY RATIONS<<<<<<<<<<<

It's horrible to arrive at your vacation location after-hours with kids who are hungry. I always travel with two cans of soup, some ramen noodles, and granola or protein bars. More than once my stash has saved the day.

Lisa Bergren, Colorado Springs, Colo.

INSIDER ADVICE If you think you'll be returning to a hotel, ask the housekeeping staff what the best rooms are. They really know, and if a room is empty they'll often show it to you. Write down the room number and request it the next time you make a reservation or when you check in.

George Green, Houston, Tex.

EASY AS PIE To feed a family of four in an expensive tropical location like Anguilla or Bermuda (or most other Caribbean locations, for that matter), ask if your hotel has phone books and, if so, look up the local pizza place. The restaurants will nearly always deliver for free.

Bianca Mims, Houston, Tex.

SAFE TIPS Whenever we stay in a hotel, I put the house-cleaning tips inside the room safe as soon as we check in. That way I don't have to worry about looking for extra dollars before we leave for sightseeing trips. I just pull the day's housekeeping tip out of the safe, and we're ready to go.

Christine Polaschek, Garland, Tex.

TWOFER To leave our hotel room on time, I request two wake-up calls: the first for when we need to get up, and the second for when we should be walking out the door.

Scott W. Ball, San Antonio, Tex.

LIVE LIKE A LOCAL<<<<<<<

If you own a time-share and pay property taxes on it, you probably qualify for a local library card. Just bring a photo ID and a copy of your property-tax receipt. While on vacation, you'll be able to check out books, DVDs, and CDs from your new "local" library.

Joe and Kathleen Weber, Missoula, Mont.

BRING THE NOISE<<<<<<

We always travel with a sound machine. When the hotel walls are thin or our room is close to an elevator, the white-noise setting is just enough to buffer outside commotions—and to save our family from a sleepless night.

Jane Tague, Fort Myers, Fla.

GET A GRIP<<<<<<<<<<<<<

Our hotel in Costa Rica had a beautiful marble shower with a very slippery floor. We laid one of our towels on the shower floor and turned on the water. Once the towel was soaking wet, it made for the perfect slip-proof surface.

Shelley Molnar, Warren, N.J.

PILLOW TALK If you like to bring your own pillows when traveling but don't want to risk leaving them behind, buy pillowcases in a design or color you would never find in a hotel.

Molly Rogers, Redondo Beach, Calif.

MEMBERS ONLY Sign up for guest programs at every hotel chain that offers one, even if you've never stayed there or think you may not travel enough to reap rewards. Some programs send coupons for discounted rooms or complimentary upgrades just for being a member. After signing up for the Omni Hotels Select Guest program, I received a coupon that I was able to redeem for a room in Chicago for $80 per night.

Allison Meyer, Chicago, Ill.

CHERCHEZ LE SHOE<<<<<<<

If you've ever checked out of a hotel only to find that you left your family's tickets, money, or other things in the room safe, lay out your clothes the night before, putting one of the shoes you're planning to wear inside or on top of the safe. There's no way you'll be able to walk away without your shoe—or your valuables.

Ellen Schollenberger, Redlands, Calif.

CHAPTER SEVEN

【29 20 002】

AT YOUR DESTINATION: **7**

EXPLORING

MADE EASY ‹‹‹‹

BUDGET TRAVEL

ART SMARTS At museums, my husband and I always ask the ticket agent if treasure hunts are offered. Some museums, like the Van Gogh Museum in Amsterdam, have a list of specific works that are interesting to kids. It's also easy to stage your own hunt: Stop at the gift shop and let everyone select postcards of the art they want to discover.

Susan Weaver, Ghlin, Belgium

BADGE OF HONOR Nearly every U.S. national park and historic site has a badge or patch that kids can earn through the nationwide Junior Ranger Program. On a recent trip to Boston, our Cub Scout earned three Scout Ranger badges and seven Junior Ranger badges.

R. Ted Jeo, Maplewood, Minn.

A POOL OF ONE'S OWN<<<<<<

I'm an avid surfer, but my young son
is afraid of even the lightest chops.
To keep everyone happy at the beach,
I buy a plastic tarp; excavate a broad,
shallow hole in the sand; line the hole
with the tarp; and fill the liner with
ocean water to create an instant
wading pool. The water is so shallow
that it heats up quickly in the sun
and can be easily tossed in the event
of an "accident."

Mike McCormack, New York, N.Y.

CREATIVE SOLUTION When visiting museums, we give each of our children a sketch pad and a pencil and invite them to draw their favorite piece. When they look back at their work, they discuss it as if they were real critics!

Ashleigh Hodges, Hercules, Calif.

MEMBERSHIP HAS ITS PRIVILEGES If your travels take you to American cities large enough to have museums, zoos, or botanical gardens, consider buying a membership in your home city's counterpart. Many have reciprocal privileges with institutions elsewhere. A membership at Chicago's Lincoln Park Zoo, for example, gains entry to zoos in Los Angeles, Des Moines, and Jackson, Miss., all at no charge.

Alice M. Solovy, Skokie, Ill.

BUDGETING LESSONS To avoid the "Can I have . . . ?" questions, set a trip allowance and stick to it. Upon arriving, we give our kids their souvenir money for the whole trip, and it's up to them to spend it wisely.

Nadine MacLane, Seattle, Wash.

LOCAL FARE No matter where we go with our four kids, ages 10 to 19, we always try to eat somewhere or do something as a local would, to get a real feel for the place. On a cruise stop in Ocho Rios, Jamaica, a Jamaican waiter advised us to contact his pastor, who took us on a tour in the church van. We loved it!

Pamela Barry, Newtown, Pa.

LITERARY COMPASS Visit a children's bookstore or the children's section of a large bookstore in your destination for some of the best advice. We've found that "book people" generally know their community very well, and the staff—and often other customers—are always happy to help.

Bill Rosberg, Cedar Rapids, Iowa

SEAT SAVER Looking for Broadway discounts? As an alternative to the TKTS booths, where you could spend half the day waiting in line, check out broadwaybox.com. This site gives discount codes that result in up to $50 off box-office prices. For example, we found $39 tickets for *Mary Poppins* that would have cost $62.

Grace Bulanan, Daly City, Calif.

RIDE ON! Many large department and discount stores sell several styles of bicycles for kids and adults, usually costing under $100. If you're planning to stay at least a week in a destination, it might pay off to buy rather than rent. At the end of your trip, you can donate the wheels to a local thrift shop for a tax write-off.

Foster Rains, Agoura, Calif.

BEACHY CLEAN When heading to the beach, we put a damp washcloth in a Ziploc bag and keep it in our cooler. It's an instant refresher, and it's ideal for removing sand and saltwater residue.

Sharon McCormac, Richmond, Ind.

INCENTIVE PLAN<<<<<<<

On past trips to Yellowstone and Alaska, to keep our crew interested in the scenery during long hikes and drives, we set rewards for spotting animals. An antelope was worth $10, and the bounty on a hard-to-find moose was $12.

Debby Schlesinger, Granda Hills, Calif.

A LIFT FOR LESS The next time you plan a skiing trip to Summit County, Colo., buy your lift tickets in Denver instead of waiting until arriving at the resorts. Discounted tickets for Breckenridge, Keystone, Arapahoe Basin, Copper Mountain, and others are sold at local grocery stores and sports shops.

Wendy Kunze, Clinton Township, Mich.

SHADOW PLAY On a visit to New York City, when our three young kids started to flag from so much walking, I made up the game of "chasing shadows": One person would run a bit ahead and the others would race to catch the leader's shadow. We managed to cover a lot of distance in a very fun way.

Carol Fisher, Flagler Beach, Fla.

CIRCULATE, PEOPLE If you're on a group tour with several family members or friends, try not to sit together at every meal or bus ride. You'll have a much better time if you occasionally split up and engage fellow travelers.

Kay Gleason, Athol, Mass.

ANY WAY YOU SLICE IT On a recent picnic, my husband forgot to pack a knife. I had a container of dental floss in my purse, so I used the floss to slice our cheese and our cake. It worked! The picnic was saved, and there were no messy knives to clean up afterward.

Florem Hill, Lake Elsinore, Calif.

PARK IT<<<<<<<<<<<<<<<

When my husband and I travel abroad with our kids, we always plan to spend a day at a local zoo or amusement park about midway through the trip. Our kids really appreciate taking a break from all the museums and monuments!

Gwen Gibbons, Thousand Oaks, Calif.

YE SHALL RECEIVE<<<<<<<

On a recent trip to Tucson, I asked the woman at the visitors' information center if she had any two-for-one coupons for area attractions. She did even better, producing two free tickets to the next day's spring-training baseball game at Tucson Electric Park.

Charlie Tiebout, Seattle, Wash.

EAT UP THE VIEW If you plan to visit the sky deck of a tall building such as Chicago's John Hancock Center or Seattle's Space Needle, find out if there's a restaurant at or near the top. Customers usually don't have to pay to get into the building and can enjoy dinner or drinks with a view.

Joyce Porter, Oak Park, Ill.

GOLD STAR FOR GOLDEN STAR Go to goldstar.com for half-price tickets to shows and events in such cities as Boston, Chicago, Los Angeles, New York, San Diego, San Francisco, San Jose, Washington, D.C., and others. Membership is free, and it enables you to buy tickets online and pick them up at the will-call window. I used the site to get half-price tickets to *The Phantom of the Opera* and *Mamma Mia!* in Las Vegas.

Kevin Lum, San Francisco, Calif.

EASY ACCESS Some popular museums have secondary entrances. The Louvre, for instance, has an alternate entrance to the famous glass pyramid at the Carrousel du Louvre, usually mobbed with crowds. To find these lesser-known entrances, search online using the museum name and the words "alternate entrance."

Susan Lore, Chesterfield, Mo.

FISHING FOR INFO The U.S. Fish and Wildlife Service (fws.gov) is a great resource for learning about kid-friendly environmental programs. In southeast Tennessee, for example, look into joining a freshwater biologist on an underwater fish-viewing excursion in the Conasauga River; in Colorado your family can take part in a wildlife-watch workshop.

Sherel Purcell, Toronto, Ont.

SAND-FREE SOLUTION Take along a container of baby powder the next time you go to the beach. Before getting back into your car, sprinkle powder on everyone's feet. The sand falls right off!

Christine DeFrehn, Mercerville, N.J.

THE MAILMAN KNOWS While searching for our bed-and-breakfast in York, England, we became hopelessly lost. On the outskirts of the city, we happened upon a small convenience store with a post office and asked for help. The postal worker quickly drew us a detailed map. There must have been a dozen turns, but we arrived safely—and greatly relieved—at our destination. Now, wherever we go, we know whom to ask for directions.

Kay Farrimond, Petoskey, Mich.

SCIENTIFIC GENIUS If you have a membership to your local science museum and it's a part of the Association of Science-Technology Centers, you can get free admission to hundreds of its affiliates throughout the country, such as L.A.'s Natural History Museum and the Chicago Children's Museum. In the past year, we've visited eight museums with our children and have saved more than $500 in entrance fees.

Linda Holt, Camden, Maine

A MOVIE A DAY I understand wanting your kids to absorb culture and scenery during vacations, but there comes a point in every day when they're just plain done. Bring a small portable DVD player and let them watch a movie. You'll all get much more out of the other 22 hours you have together.

Lisa Bergren, Colorado Springs, Colo.

CHAPTER EIGHT

SAFETY PATROL:

KEEPING YOUR CLAN SECURE

8

INSTANT ID BRACELETS I write my cell phone number on the inside of rubber bracelets (such as the ones for Lance Armstrong's foundation) and have my children wear them when we're away from home. That way, should we get separated, they can show the number to a helpful adult. You can also slip the information on a piece of paper they keep in their pocket—but the bracelets don't get lost as easily.

Susan Redman, Hebron, Conn.

NO OUTLET If you're traveling with small kids, bring a pack of plastic electrical-outlet inserts. When our daughter was young, we used them in hotels, cabins, and non-baby-proofed houses, and they brought us much peace of mind. In a pinch, placing Scotch tape or duct tape over outlets also does the trick.

Robin Hemenway, St. Paul, Minn.

TWEETING Give your children a coach's whistle to wear around their necks. If they get lost or come in harm's way, the piercing sound will definitely help you find them more quickly.

Chandra Huang, Honolulu, Hawaii

CAMERA READY While on vacation, I take a digital photo of our daughter each day so that if she gets lost, I have a picture that shows exactly what she's wearing.

Stacy Walker, Terry, Miss.

ESSENTIAL ADVICE<<<<<<<

When we stay in a hotel, I keep our money, passport, cell phone, camera, and all other important items in a tote bag by the bed. In an emergency, I can just grab the tote with everything we need. I came up with this trick when I was staying in a hotel and the fire alarm sounded in the middle of the night.

Dana Seifner, Baden, Pa.

STEAL TRAP Our bags have been stolen twice from inside locked rental cars. Now we travel with a bicycle cable and lock. If we absolutely have to leave our suitcases in the car, I hook them together by the handles and attach the whole thing to the car frame. Even if thieves manage to get in, the cable will slow them down.

Karen McCarty, McCall, Idaho

1-800-NO-GO Before traveling overseas, look at your health insurance card. If it shows only an 800 or 888 number for precertification of hospital admissions, call that number and obtain the local number with an area code. Many 800 numbers can't be dialed from foreign countries. I learned this the hard way during an emergency hospital admission in Switzerland. I could have avoided the delay in reaching my carrier.

Chris Carveth, Orange, Conn.

INFO-SHARE We always e-mail our itinerary—including flights, hotels, and confirmation numbers—to ourselves and to family members. If our luggage is lost or our wallets are stolen, all the essential information is just a few quick clicks away.

Courtney Fuller, Atlanta, Ga.

SUBWAY PLAN B A common family-travel nightmare involves subway doors closing before everyone in the group manages to get on. As a contingency plan, tell your gang to get off at the next stop and wait for the others.

Ludivina García, Monterrey, Mexico

THE BEST POLICY Squaremouth.com provides comparable details on more than 250 travel-insurance plans, enabling you to make the best choice. Insurance companies are allowed to be part of its extensive lineup only if they've met the standards of industry overseers such as A.M. Best and state insurance commissioners.

Marc Oppy, Portland, Ore.

SAFETY IN A SNAP Ever since my children were small, I've carried recent, wallet-size photos of them when we all go on vacation, in case we get separated. Now that they're teenagers and traveling with friends' families, too, I send pictures for the other family to bring along. I also write my telephone numbers on the back of the pictures so that they know where to reach me in an emergency.

Ruth Ann Newsum, Hutchinson, Kans.

SOUND THE ALARM If you're staying at a single-story motel with outside doors and you're concerned about security, keep your car keys on the nightstand and park near your room. If it appears that someone is trying to get into your room, all you have to do is press the panic button on the car key and the car's honking should chase away the intruder.

Dick Boardman, Fairport, N.Y.

WAY TO GO Whenever we travel, especially in foreign countries, we always make certain that our children, ages 9 and 12, have a hotel business card in their pockets along with our contact numbers. That way, if we get separated, the police know right where to take them and how to let us know they're safe.

Sandy and John Bagan, Thousand Oaks, Calif.

CHAPTER NINE

PLANET AMUSEMENT PARK: 09

TO DISNEY AND BEYOND

BUDGET TRAVEL

BIG-BOX BARGAINS When you're on vacation in southern California, check out a local Costco for discount tickets to theme parks such as Universal Studios, Legoland, and the San Diego Zoo.

Michele Sinclair, Playa del Rey, Calif.

COLOR GUARD To ease your trip through a big park like Disneyland, dress everyone in your group in T-shirts in the same eye-catching color so you'll be sure to spot them in a crowd.

Ludivina García, Monterrey, Mexico

QUICK LIKE A MOUSE<<<<<<

You'll save time—and money—by visiting your local Disney Store ahead of time to buy tickets for your trip to Walt Disney World or Disneyland.

Ed Tucker, Fremont, Calif.

REWARDING GOOD BEHAVIOR Before driving with their two boys to Walt Disney World, our daughter and son-in-law went to the local Disney Store and purchased Disney Dollars. In the months leading up to the trip, the boys received Disney Dollars when they were good. The boys were then able to buy their own souvenirs at the store in the park, which felt like a real reward.

Darlene Burrough, Thorofare, N.J.

FAST TRACK I'm a former travel-industry professional based in Orlando, and this is my best secret for getting around town without delays: Avoid the eternally congested International Drive and take Universal Boulevard instead. It runs parallel to I-Drive, but the comparisons end there.

Janey Womeldorf, Orlando, Fla.

GET CARDED<<<<<<<<<<<<<<

You can get discounts on admission tickets and hotel stays at any Disney park—plus free stroller rentals—if you've accumulated points on a Disney Rewards Visa card. To redeem the points, just be sure to request your rewards at least six weeks in advance.

Kristi Kosloske, Chicago, Ill.

SLIP 'EM A MICKEY<<<<<<<

Before we visit Walt Disney World, I buy Disney items from a local discount store. Once at the park, I tell my daughter that if she's good, she'll get a surprise back at the room. Then I give her a Disney souvenir, but at a fraction of the cost!

Stacy Walker, Terry, Miss.

DRENCHED BUT DRY If you plan to visit a theme park, always bring a few sandwich-size plastic bags. They'll protect your cell phone and your wallet when you're riding on flumes and other water attractions.

Jack Bell, Kissimmee, Fla.

PACK IT IN Get each family member a fanny pack and let them fill it with snacks of their choosing. You won't get stuck in line at kiosks or have to pay for overpriced park food.

Doug Rittenhouse, Port Angeles, Wash.

SURF FOR SAVINGS I always check Craigslist and eBay to see if I can find discounted tickets and coupons. I've located some great deals on these sites. Just make sure the tickets or coupons are transferable and haven't expired.

Perry Babel, Lakewood, Colo.

LEARN TO SHARE There are lots of time-share resorts in the Orlando area, and you don't have to be a member to stay in them. They usually cost less than a hotel, have larger rooms, and are in complexes with game rooms, fitness centers, and convenience stores. Look for listings on redweek.com, where time-share owners post the weeks they want to sell.

Bethany Edmunds, Selinsgrove, Pa.

PACKING SOME POWDER Buying the whole family drinks in theme parks is expensive. So I carry those powdered to-go packets of ice tea, lemonade, or Kool-Aid. All I have to do is fill up a water bottle, add the mix, and, voilà, instant refreshment.

Maribelle Loria, Reno, Nev.

AAA-OK I've saved lots of money using AAA. In addition to providing roadside services, most AAA chapters offer discounted tickets to Walt Disney World and a preferred parking pass that enables you to grab specially designated spots near the entrances. It's a dollar saver, and you don't have to walk far or take the trolley in the parks.

Judy Small, Cicero, Ind.

PHOTOGRAPHIC PROOF If you sign up for Disney's PhotoPass card, which gives you access to the shots the park photographers take of you and your family, make sure to snap a picture of the code on the back. We lost our card on our third day, but because we had taken a picture of the code, the park was able to transfer our info to a new card right away.

Stella Brewer, New York, N.Y.

FRONT-ROW SEATS On our trips to Walt Disney World, we like to ride in the front of the Monorail. Simply tell the Disney cast member that you would like to wait for the front, and he or she will send you to a special gated area. Though there's no guarantee, be patient and chances are you'll be seated with the driver (limit four guests), where you can ask questions. And you'll receive a Monorail System Co-Pilot License at the end of your trip!

Carey Clamens, Hilton Head Island, S.C.

CLEAN GETAWAY If you have an evening flight out of Orlando and want to visit one last theme park during the day, make it Discovery Cove. With its tropical birds, beaches, and dolphin swims, the park is fabulous (if pricey) for all ages. Better still, it has showers and basic toiletries for guests, so everyone can freshen up before the flight.

Marc Smith, Austin, Tex.

ALL BOTTLED UP The last time we went to Walt Disney World, we had two 24-count cases of bottled water delivered to the hotel's front desk before we arrived. Instead of shelling out $2 or $3 per bottle in the parks, we paid a total of $12 for both cases. You can order them from chain stores such as Staples. You can also bring your own water bottles and refill them at drinking fountains in the parks.

Patricia Spillane, Warwick, R.I.

TIE ONE ON Loop a brightly colored scarf around the handle of your stroller before entering a ride. When you return, you'll quickly pick out your stroller from a sea of look-alikes.

Katrina Shelton, Beaumont, Tex.

EXIT STRATEGY Many families stay at amusement parks from early morning until closing time, but this often leads to tired, cranky kids (and parents). We've found it's best to return to our room in the early afternoon, when it's typically very hot and the lines are longest. We eat a quick lunch, take a swim in the pool, and nap for a couple of hours. Then we return to the park. As closing time nears, the weather is cooler, the lines are almost always shorter (especially for the kiddie rides), and we're refreshed.

Ken Ferris, DuPont, Wash.

CHAPTER TEN

THE VACATION
AT SEA:

CRUISING
WITH YOUR
CREW

10

SLUMBER PARTY! When on a cruise with our two toddlers, we usually book a cabin with four twin beds (two lower and two upper). None of us are comfortable in the upper bunks, so we push the two lower beds together and sleep sideways. That way, the four of us fit comfortably. One parent sleeps at the bottom edge of the beds, acting as a rail to prevent the kids from rolling off.

Jimmy Kung, Brooklyn, N.Y.

SHIPPING NEWS A must for cruising newbies is to read the discussion boards at cruisecritic.com (and disboards.com for Disney cruises). They cover almost every detail, including traveling with kids, choosing the right cabin, up-to-date dinner menus, and worthy excursions. You don't have to register unless you want to ask a question. Just search for the cruise line and the ship you'll be on.

Brenda Chen, Lawrenceville, N.J.

KEY TRACKER We always book several cabins and request multiple key cards for each. I bring stick-on dots (the ones from office-supply stores) and establish a different color for each room. I put a colored dot on the door lock and dots of the same color on the key cards for that room. The dots peel right off when we leave.

Lila Held, Garden Grove, Calif.

PREP SCHOOL I make individually numbered, dated, and labeled Ziploc bags for each port of call. The packets contain excursion-specific items—such as a downloaded local map, sunscreen, insect repellent, itinerary and proof of reservations, a disposable camera labeled with each port's name, and items like shampoo samples for the spots where we have swimming activities planned.

Deborah Plumb, St. Petersburg, Fla.

ONE FOR THE AGES Double-check the age requirements for your cruise line's kids' program. My daughter was two weeks shy of the minimum cutoff, and our travel agent said she'd be allowed to participate if she was potty trained. Turned out the age limit was firm, and we wished we'd stayed put.

Gayle Forman, Brooklyn, N.Y.

GO YOUR OWN WAY Royal Caribbean could have transported our family of four from Houston to the Port of Galveston in Texas before our cruise, but I found the fee pretty expensive. Instead, I searched car-rental-company Web sites and booked a car for a reasonable rate. I then found prepaid parking at the Port of Galveston. Even after paying for a car rental and a week of parking, we saved more than $120.

Jeanette Boyd, Richland, Mo.

ROGER THAT! Bring along battery-operated two-way radios such as Motorola's Talkabouts to keep everyone connected. Typically used for skiing, they worked great on our last family cruise.

Sherry Brooks, Westlake Village, Calif.

CRUISERS ARE CLUBBERS If you're new to a major line such as Carnival or Princess, be sure you check out its frequent-cruiser program before you set sail. We've received access to a priority line for nightly shows (instead of standing and waiting with everyone else), and on one cruise we returned to our cabin to discover a plate of chocolate-covered strawberries.

Steve Maglich, Rolling Meadows, Ill.

STEER CLEAR OF NOISE<<<<

Before booking a specific cabin, go to the ship's deck plans on the cruise line's Web site and make certain your quarters won't be directly under a heavily traveled area. Many Princess ships, for example, have a 24-hour buffet on the Lido Deck; diners get their food and take it to a poolside area over cabins on the Aloha Deck, on both the starboard and port sides. The Lido Deck has a wood floor, and when chairs are dragged, the noise just might send you overboard.

N. W. Pope, Scottsdale, Ariz.

BABY MONITORS FOR BIG KIDS Families have trouble finding affordable staterooms that sleep more than four, and connecting rooms usually require you to book two rooms of the same category. Well, we're off on our fourth cruise and here's what we do: My husband and I stay in an ocean-view cabin, and our three kids are in a cabin across the hall. I bring a baby monitor that I bought at a garage sale and use it to listen to my kids' room. I can sleep knowing I'll be in their room the minute I hear a "Mom, I need you!" Plus we get two bathrooms, extra closet space, and plenty of room to roam.

Penny Laschanzky, Lincoln, Nebr.

HELLO YELLOW Bring a highlighter, and when you get your four-page activities sheet, you can mark all the events you want to attend instead of going back to the sheet and trying to find them among all the ones listed.

Mike Gerstenberger, Pearland, Tex.

ELIMINATE THE MIDDLEMAN Cruise lines offer packaged side trips at their ports of call. If you go online and look for these expeditions ahead of time, you can book directly with the tour companies and save money.

Cindy Rucker, Jekyll Island, Ga.

STATEROOMY We love going on cruises, but we don't love the cramped cabins. We've discovered that if we use rolling duffel bags instead of traditional suitcases, we can collapse and store them under the beds after we unpack. The bags no longer hog our valuable space.

Carole Sondike, Deerfield Beach, Fla.

AMASSING POWER Be sure to pack a power strip and an extension cord. Many ship cabins have only one outlet, but you'll definitely need more if you want to use your family's laptop, iPods, cell phones, electric razor, and hairdryer.

Jay Van Vechten, Boca Raton, Fla.

EXTRA CREDIT Before you book a cruise, find out if the line offers benefits for signing up for its credit card. For example, Carnival offers a card that lets you earn points that can be put toward future cruises, resort stays, and air travel.

Paula Prindle, Orient, Ohio

CRUISE CONTROL Because of a late connecting flight, my family and I missed our cruise's departure from Miami. The cruise line offered to fly us to the ship's first scheduled port to join our group a few days later, but we didn't want to miss so much time at sea. Our solution: We asked the cruise line if we could join a different cruise leaving from Miami the next day. The company obliged, and we had a wonderful trip. It never hurts to ask!

Mary Myers, Erie, Colo.

HOT ROD Since ships' cabins are notorious for having minimal closet space, we always pack a tension rod. We set it up between the TV stand and the wall by the porthole, window, or balcony door to fashion a second closet.

Lisa Palumbo, West Orange, N.J.

TUNE IN TO ISLAND LIFE Bring a portable AM/FM radio when you go on a Caribbean cruise. You'll be amazed at the interesting stations you'll receive while on the ship (AM radio signals travel easily over open water). Reggae, salsa, merengue, compas, zouk—the list of genres goes on and on. Plus, news and commercials on small island stations can be quite entertaining.

Tom Roche, Tucker, Ga.

SEA HOW WE WORK IT Before going on a cruise, we visit our local souvenir shop and put together a small gift bag. We include postcards and magnets and also regional specialties, such as cactus candy. When we get to our cabin, we give the present to our attendant, who's usually delighted—and rewards us with great service.

Nyal R. Cammack, Las Cruces, N.M.

BAR NONE If your cabin refrigerator is an honor bar stocked with stuff you don't intend to purchase, ask your steward to remove everything. You'll have more space for your own items, and it'll be a lot harder for the cruise line to mistakenly charge you for drinks and snacks you didn't take.

Ray A. Evon, Daytona Beach, Fla.

SHOE-IN A shoe organizer hung over the bathroom door is my solution for hotel-room or stateroom clutter. The compartments are perfect for stashing toiletries, sunblock, sunglasses, travel docs, and, of course, shoes. The extra storage space came in especially handy on a recent cruise, when we needed all the room we could get in our tiny cabin.

Jane Tague, Westerville, Ohio

STEAM CLEAN On most cruise lines, you have to pay for spa treatments, but on some ships, you can use the spa's showers and steam rooms for free. After my daughter and I work out and have a steam session on a cruise, we forgo the tiny showers in our staterooms for the spacious ones in the spa. Also, a lot of spas have relaxation rooms that are sometimes open to any cruiser who wants to get away from the action.

April Icsman, Medina, Ohio

SHED YOUR BAGGAGE If you choose a Holland America cruise, ask whether the ship offers Signature Express Baggage Service. For $16 per person, the company prints your boarding passes the day before disembarkation and transports your luggage directly to your airline the morning of your flight. This is a godsend when you're herding a family. No worries about baggage check; just report directly to your gate.

Jeanette Parker, Lafayette, La.

165

Cruising with Your Crew

LOST AT SEA? Every time we go on a cruise, my wife blows up a red balloon and tapes it to the door of our stateroom. We never have any trouble finding our way in the ship's long hallways.

Eli Rose, Tampa, Fla.

DISCOUNT SPA DAY I've been on many cruises with various lines, and I've learned that the spas usually offer discounts on days when the ship is docked. So while one parent takes the kids on an excursion, the other can sign up for a massage!

Rhonda Grabov, Philadelphia, Pa.

CHAPTER ELEVEN

BUDGET TRAVEL
11

FOREIGN DESTINATIONS:
FINDING YOUR WAY IN EXOTIC PLACES

FOOTBALL DIPLOMACY We brought a small football on a backpacking trip through Europe and were amazed by the number of curious onlookers. Tossing the ball around is a great way to interact with locals, especially when there's a language barrier. Plus, you can easily leave an inexpensive ball behind as a gift to a lucky child—and you'll have more room in your bag for souvenirs.

Mason Swartz, Racine, Wis.

S.O.S. In the U.S., we know to dial 911 in emergencies, but other countries use different numbers. For that reason, the GSM phone systems have created a single emergency number: 112. If you dial 112 from a GSM phone in several countries, including the U.K., Australia, Singapore, and all other spots in the EU, you'll be immediately connected to emergency services.

Alan Brill, Staten Island, N.Y.

SINGLED OUT If you're divorced and plan to travel out of the country with your children, check the legal requirements in advance. When I tried to take my kids to Cancún, I learned too late that Mexico requires a notarized letter of consent signed by both parents, or a copy of the parental custody agreement, for minors traveling alone or with one parent or guardian. The airlines all enforce this rule now, before you get on the plane.

Marge Stratton, Big Flats, N.Y.

JAPANESE EASE While traveling in Japan with our six children one summer, my wife and I discovered a way to reduce our lunch and dinner expenses. Almost every Japanese department store offers a selection of precooked meals to take home to eat. The food was wonderful, our children could choose things that interested them, and the experience was purely Japanese. The food emporiums are usually found in the basement—not to be confused with the pricier restaurants located on the top floors of most department stores.

Ralph Ellsworth, San Juan Capistrano, Calif.

JUST PRESS PLAY Instead of taking guided tours in Rome, I downloaded a series of self-guided audio tours for MP3 players from SoundGuides (sound-guides.com). The company has complete programs for Venice, Paris, and London as well as special versions of the London and Rome tours for kids.

Monica J. Pileggi, Frederick, Md.

QUID YOU NOT I discovered a great Web site while my family and I were living in London: freelondonlistings.co.uk. It lists events and attractions around the city that are completely (or nearly) free.

Peggy Bennett, West Hartford, Conn.

BARGAIN BUS Inside most hotels in Cancún are tour-operator desks selling day trips to archaeological sites such as Chichén Itzá and Tulum. Instead of shelling out big bucks, take a local bus to the downtown station and buy a round-trip ticket for less than $10. The buses are air-conditioned and allow you to explore at your own pace. You can also arrive way ahead of the crowds.

Lolly Pineda, Millbrae, Calif.

AUF WIEDERSEHEN, BOREDOM Germany has many amusement parks, most of which aren't included in guidebooks geared for adults. And some beer gardens even have playgrounds!

Nadine MacLane, Seattle, Wash.

ID YOUR ID We have four passports to keep track of when our family travels, and we used to waste time at security trying to figure out whose was whose. Finally, I put the label maker to good use and stuck our first names onto the front of each.

Mary-Jeanine Ibarguen, Altamonte Springs, Fla.

ROYAL SAVINGS If you're heading to London and plan to spend time touring castles, it pays to become a member of the not-for-profit Historic Royal Palaces (hrp.org.uk). You'll get in free to five of the city's most impressive landmarks, including the Tower of London, Kensington Palace, and Kew Palace. Flash your card to bypass long lines and visit unlimited times within a year. Membership for a family with one adult is $79 and for one with two adults is $110. Visit just two places, and you cover almost 100 percent of the cost. Also, you get 10 percent off at the restaurants, cafés, and shops.

Tarryn Rivkin, San Jose, Calif.

DECLINE LIKE A LOCAL<<<<

Several years ago we were quite
bothered by street sellers in Turkey.
We kept repeating "No, thank you"
in English, to no avail. We decided
to learn to say it in Turkish. An old
gentleman trying to sell us his wares
replied, in English, "Ah, you speak
Turkish." He smiled and immediately
went on his way. This friendly tactic
has also worked in India.

William Wilson, Kailua, Hawaii

BETTER SAFE THAN SORRY If you have an early flight, it's a smart idea to make sure your hotel-room safe is unlocked before going to sleep. Recently, the evening before departure we tried to open our room safe (which contained passports and other valuables), but it wouldn't budge—and the receptionist had no idea of the code to unlock it! If we had waited until the morning, we never would have made our flight.

Sandra DeGroot, Grand Haven, Mich.

WAY TO GO Renting an apartment abroad is a great alternative to staying in hotels, especially for families. Just be sure to take a map and detailed directions, particularly if you don't speak the language. We encountered taxi drivers in Brussels, Madrid, Seville, and Palermo who had no idea how to find our apartments' addresses.

Gary Maier, New Westminster, B.C.

FOOD FOR THOUGHT When we take our kids to foreign destinations, in addition to spending days at museums, cathedrals, and castles, we visit supermarkets and department stores. We learn a lot about each culture by perusing the aisles. Some food is odd to us, some is familiar, and we always buy something new to try.

Gwen Gibbons, Thousand Oaks, Calif.

BANK ON IT Before traveling to another country, be sure to visit bank-holidays.com to find out when businesses there are closed and what types of holidays might be taking place. You may be lucky enough to catch some local celebrations.

Elisabeth Smith, Los Angeles, Calif.

SITE SAVVY Admission to many of Ireland's historic sites can really add up. Buy the Heritage Card, good for unlimited admission for one year to more than 70 heritage sites across the country (including Dublin and Kilkenny castles). The card costs $28 for adults, $11 for students and children, and $73 for families. You can buy them in advance at heritageireland.ie.

Nuala Barner, Westwood, Mass.

DUCK THE COVER CHARGE If you're looking for a place to eat in Italy, check to see if the restaurant has a *coperto*, or cover charge. If you want only a light breakfast or lunch, skip the sit-down places, buy a pastry or a panini from a bakery, and picnic by a fountain or sightsee while you eat.

Blair Sechrest, Cary, N.C.

ALONE AT LAST We noticed that tour buses in western Ireland start heading back inland by 4:30 p.m. But in summer, the sun doesn't set until around 10 p.m. If you start driving the Ring of Kerry at 4 p.m., you'll still have hours of daylight to see cliffs, castles, abbeys, and forts—all with little traffic and no crowds.

Joe Quinn, Brooklyn Park, Minn.

SHOW AND CELL Asking for help in another country can be tricky, but traveling with a camera phone has made it easier. I've created a photo album with pictures of basic necessities like a bottle of water, a toilet, a taxi, and stamps. Now when I don't know the word for what I need, I just show a local the picture of it on my phone.

Jena Persico, Arlington, Va.

FRIENDS IN FLORENCE Buy a Friends of the Uffizi Gallery pass before you go to Florence (florenceforfun.org). Family membership costs $133 for two adults and two children and is good for a year. It covers the entry fee to the Uffizi and several other attractions, including the state museums of Florence, the Pitti Palace, the Medici Chapels, and more. The best part is that you get to skip ticket lines, which can be extra long in the height of summer.

Mary Davis, New Port Richey, Fla.

SAFE DRIVING When traveling in Europe by car, use the Web site Map24 (uk.map24.com) to help figure out driving directions. The directions are meant for European roads, so you'll see symbols and references that correspond with actual road signs. Very helpful.

Jimmie Price, Katy, Tex.

PALACE INTRIGUE My kids don't want to hear my history lectures, but they're fans of the audio tours offered at many museums and monuments throughout Europe, especially those available on iPods. At 10 and 12 years old, both kids were fascinated by Berlin's Charlottenburg Palace and insisted on listening to the complete (and quite long) tour. They took similar tours in France, at Chenonceau and Chambord châteaux.

Gwen Gibbons, Thousand Oaks, Calif.

HELP THEM HELP YOU Printing information from English-language Web sites for your travels is great, but make sure you also have native-language printouts with the names and locations of the places you want to visit. Locals will have an easier time showing you the way.

Margaret Lavictoire, Ottawa, Ont.

TALK IS CHEAP When traveling to Mexico, we wanted to stay in touch with family and friends back home. We found a free application on iTunes called Truphone that turns our iPhone into an Internet phone. We simply downloaded the app, bought a certain amount of time, and made calls by connecting through our resort's free Wi-Fi. We were in contact with everyone for just a few cents a minute.

Wil Cuyco, Oakland, Calif.

ITALY WITHOUT THE WAIT On a recent trip to Venice, we were able to bypass the extremely long line at St. Mark's Basilica by reserving an appointment time, for free, several days in advance (alata.it/eng/musei/musei.asp). I felt a little guilty about not waiting for an hour like everybody else, but I got over it!

Richard Drake, Waldwick, N.J.

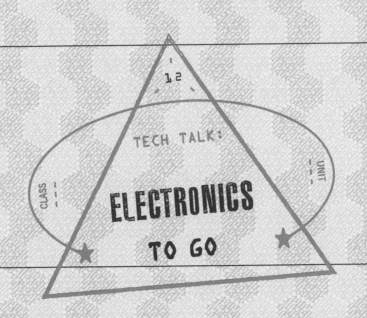

12

TECH TALK:

CLASS

UNIT

ELECTRONICS

TO GO

ADVANCE PHOTO PLANNING Before leaving on a lengthy trip, we organize ourselves photo-wise. First, we create a heading for the vacation, such as "Christmas Cruise 2009," listing ports of call and other special aspects of the trip. Then we take a clean one-gigabyte memory card and photograph a Title Shot as the first image on the card. The image acts as a title for our computer folder when we archive the pictures from the trip.

Fred Dettmann, Scottsdale, Ariz.

DIGITAL DOPP KIT We store all adapters, chargers, batteries, iPods, cameras, and phones in a toiletry bag, which we call our technology bag. It's easy to grab when going on a trip, and if we have to leave it in our car, it just looks like an ordinary toiletry bag. Who breaks into a car to steal toothpaste?

Jody Kirincich, Falmouth, Mass.

BLOG WATCH By starting a blog for each trip (at blogger. com, among other sites), you can keep friends and family up-to-date on your adventures. All you need is an Internet café to add entries and photos while you're on the road.

Alan A. Lew, Flagstaff, Ariz.

A REAL FEAT Since many small digital cameras don't come with a carrying case, we slipped our Canon Elph into one of our granddaughter's toddler-size socks. A brightly colored or patterned one makes it easy to find in a purse or backpack.

Cindy Jones, Bass Lake, Calif.

INFO FLASH<<<<<<<<<<<<<

I use an inexpensive, thumb-size
USB flash drive to store medical and
insurance contacts, confirmation codes,
credit card numbers, addresses, and
phone numbers. It fits in a secure zipped
pocket in my travel purse (and I make
sure it's either password protected or
encrypted). If I don't have my laptop,
I can insert the flash drive in most
hotel or Internet café computers.

Linda Steven, Saint Paul, Minn.

NOTES TO SELF When I find travel tips online, I copy, paste, and e-mail the information to myself for future reference. A few days before a trip, I e-mail a shorter version of that information to my cell phone as a text message. Then when my family and I arrive at our destination, I have all the tips, phone numbers, and addresses stored as text messages.

Douglas Rutkowski, Tampa, Fla.

CALL IT AN ITIN Those earbud-type earphones fit perfectly into a small Altoids chewing gum tin. They stay safe and untangled, and the tin slips nicely into a pocket or purse.

Becky Sapp, Arlington, Va.

THE DOWNLOAD We recently bought a camera connector from the Apple Store that allows us to download the day's photos from our digital camera to our photo-capable iPod. It clears out the camera storage card and keeps the photos safe until we can put them on our computer back home.

Denny Huffman, Washougal, Wash.

BLUE LIGHT SPECIAL! Kmart and Sears Grand stores have computers with free Internet access at some locations in California and Hawaii (and in more than 25 other states)— handy for anyone traveling without a laptop.

Karen Carlson, Corona del Mar, Calif.

CHARGER CARD I was always forgetting my cell-phone charger in hotel rooms, leaving it next to an outlet. Finally, I wrote "charger" in big black letters on a five-by-seven index card and started keeping it in the bottom of my luggage at all times. When I open my suitcase, the first thing I remember to grab is my charger! It worked so well, I brought a bunch of index cards on my next trip and gave one to everyone. We haven't forgotten a charger since.

David P. Triche, Austin, Tex.

TALK TO YOURSELF If your digital camera has video technology, you can record an audio file after you take a picture, eliminating the need to jot down where you took a particular shot.

Pat Blizzard, Freeland, Pa.

FINDERS BEEPERS An audible electronic key finder—the kind that emits a loud beep or ring when activated—can save the day. Keep the small remote locator on you and put the receiver disc in your luggage, handbag, camera case, etc. You can press the locator button to thwart a thief trying to steal your bag. And, of course, the device can help you find your keys.

James Pennington, Portland, Ore.

ALL TOGETHER NOW After I left an iPod charger in Paris, my rechargeable camera battery in Colorado, and a computer cord in Williamsburg, Va., I decided it's worth the space to pack a power strip. Now I can recharge all our electronic equipment together, so I only have to remember one thing when I leave my hotel. Even better, when we travel internationally, I don't need a bunch of adapters.

Sharon Arnn Bryant, Batesville, Va.

FIND YOUR WAY BY PDA If you have a PDA or a Web-enabled phone, you can access subway and bus directions for Boston, Chicago, Long Island, New York City, San Francisco, Washington, D.C., and London, among other places. Go to hopstop.com/pda, choose your location, and enter an intersection or address. The service will also tell you the best way to get there using public transportation.

Lisa Levine, Hollywood, Calif.

HANDLE WITH CARE When I'm staying in a hotel, I always wrap my cell-phone charger cord around the handle of my suitcase and then put the suitcase near an electrical outlet. The bag serves as a stand for my phone while it's charging, and I never forget the charger since it's attached to the handle of the suitcase.

David Rhoads, Derwood, Md.

SEPARATION ANXIETY If you pack electronics in your carry-on, be sure to include all cords, chargers, and adapters in the same bag. When we went to Africa, we put our cameras in the carry-on, and we packed the cords in our checked baggage. Our bags didn't show up in Tanzania, however, so we had all the equipment but no way to recharge it, and we couldn't get replacements.

Andrew Fritz, Somerset, N.J.

PICASA AT SU CASA My family and I used to struggle with our pictures being too bright or out of focus—especially when we were using our cheap camera—but now we edit them with Google's free Picasa software. When we transfer our pictures to a folder on the computer, Picasa automatically detects and displays them, and we use simple buttons to crop, sharpen, or adjust the lighting in the photos. The editing process is so simple that our kids often have it done before we're even fully unpacked.

Vic Singhal, Fords, N.J.

CHAPTER THIRTEEN

BUG BITES AND OTHER BOTHERS:

TRAVEL
REMEDIES

✚

IMMIGRATION 13

<BT<<<<<<<<<<<<<<<<<<<<<<<<<<<<<<<<
9781594744488<<<<<<<<<<<<<<<<10

QUEASY DOES IT I always keep Sea-Bands, which help prevent motion sickness, in my purse. They've come in handy many times—a bus ride in Costa Rica, a whale-watching trip in Maine, and a flight that had to circle before landing.

Lisa Lowe Stauffer, Roswell, Ga.

GET CULTURED Traveling abroad often involves sampling unusual food, which can lead to stomach problems. Yogurt with probiotics, like *L. acidophilus*, helps prevent food poisoning and aids digestion. We eat some as soon as we arrive.

Kevin McCalmon, Broomfield, Colo.

BOUNCE 'EM! I've found dryer sheets to be useful in preventing ant infestations. Place them in the bugs' path or entry point, and the chemical in the sheets will prevent the ants' olfactory sensors from following their pheromone trails.

Dindo Carrillo, Fountain Valley, Calif.

DOCTOR KIT When traveling with my kids, I bring a Ziploc bag that includes four things: Benadryl, children's ibuprofen, one of those little medicine measuring cups, and a thermometer. This all-purpose kit will help with minor ailments or treat a more serious flu until you can get to a doctor. Best of all, it saves Dad from driving around at 2 A.M. looking for an all-night pharmacy.

Heather Crow, Rio Rancho, N.M.

ACT BEFORE YOU REACT If someone in your family has serious allergies, traveling to a country where you don't speak the language is scary. At selectwisely.com, you can order allergy and emergency cards in several languages and even add pictures to help communicate what you need.

Robin Willcox, South Hamilton, Mass.

FIRM FOOTING To avoid blisters during a hike, spray some antiperspirant on your ankles and heels just before setting out. It works just as it does under your arms—it prevents sweat, which, when combined with friction, is what usually causes the painful sores. It may sound odd, but I swear it really helps!

Rebecca Blevins, Decatur, Ga.

STING OPERATION<<<<<<<

My husband got stung by a bee while we were vacationing in Germany, and a local suggested putting toothpaste on the spot. The sting didn't swell, burn, or itch—amazing.

Marie Braatz, Thorp, Wis.

NATURE'S DRAMAMINE Besides being a tasty treat, candied ginger can help prevent or soothe motion sickness. (Some cruise ships even offer it with after-dinner mints.) We always carry a small supply in a Ziploc bag, whether we're on the road, in an airplane, or at sea.

Weyman Lew, San Francisco, Calif.

AVOID GETTING BUGGED I had heard that some South American hotels don't have window screens, and we didn't want to be kept awake at night by bugs, so I bought masking tape and two square yards of light nylon netting (the kind once used in prom dresses). We taped the netting over our open window every night. It worked like a charm. We had fresh air, and the pests stayed out.

Elfa Foldi, Milwaukee, Wis.

ON THE HIGH C'S Bring a few packets of Emergen-C powder on trips. Anytime you feel run-down from all the nonstop fun, mix a packet in a glass of water and drink up. The vitamin C helps you stay healthy, and the other vitamins and minerals keep your energy from flagging. This is for parents and for teens ages 15 and up; for kids ages 2–14, there's Emergen-C Kidz Complete, a multivitamin fizzy drink mix.

Andra Williams, South Amherst, Ohio

IT'S THE BALM I always bring a tube of natural-beeswax-based lip balm (SPF 15+) when I travel. It's almost like carrying a mini first-aid kit. It serves as a lip balm, of course, but also as an emergency sunscreen for noses, a moisturizer for the eye area, and a blister preventer for hands and feet.

Jay Hammond, Gilbert, Ariz.

OVER-THE-COUNTER ADVICE<<<

In developing countries, ask a
pharmacist for dining recommendations.
I travel often to India and love to
wander off the beaten path. It's crucial
to maintain one's health when
overseas, and I've discovered that
pharmacists can point you to clean
restaurants. They're also likely to
have a good command of English,
even in remote areas.

Carrie Zimmerman, New York, N.Y.

COOTIE CATCHER I swear by Zicam Cold Remedy Gel Swabs. Rub the Q-tips on the inside of everybody's noses before a flight. They're approved for kids over 3, and they stop all those icky germs in the recycled cabin air from sticking.

Dawn Foster, Auburn, Wash.

PATCH YOUR BAGS When camping, put a repellent patch on the bags that hold toiletries, groceries, and cooking utensils. It will keep pesky bugs at bay. The long-lasting patches also work wonders during a picnic. On a recent trip to the Costa Rican rain forest, I placed one on the bedside table each night and was the only one who woke up each morning bite-free.

Tiffany Provence, Summerville, S.C.

FOUR-LEGGED FLYERS I always make sure to inquire at check-in about animals on my flight—a wise move if any of your family members have allergies. On a trip from Montreal to Vienna, I sat in front of a person with a cat. Because the flight was sold out, they couldn't change my seat.

Mirvet Sidhom, Brossard, Q.C.

THE WIPE WAY Tired of catching colds while traveling? Take along a travel-size package of Clorox wipes. Disinfect the tray table and armrests on the airplane as well as the telephone, TV remote, and faucets in your hotel room.

Sherill Hacker, Williamston, Mich.

BUZZ OFF <<<<<<<<<<<<<

Before we travel in buggy or malarial areas, we treat all of our pants and shirts with the pesticide Permethrin, available in a concentrate from travel-supply companies. We dilute it in a spray bottle, spritz it on the clothes, and let them dry. (Never spray it directly on your skin.) The treatment lasts through six washings, and the EPA says it's safe for kids' clothes. More than once, we've remained free of bites at jungle locations while other guests suffered.

Marci Fuller, San Benito, Tex.

BREATHE EASIER If the dry air on planes irritates your sinuses, use a saline nasal spray, such as Ocean or Ayr or a generic brand, before you board. I always do, and so does my 10-year-old, allergy-prone daughter.

Frederic King, Denver, Colo.

DETERGENT DETERRENT Dab a bit of liquid laundry soap on a mosquito bite. Not only will it stop the itching immediately, but the bite will go away in a day or two. My friend taught me this while we were in Vietnam.

Elizabeth Cassidy, Chicago, Ill.

CHAPTER FOURTEEN

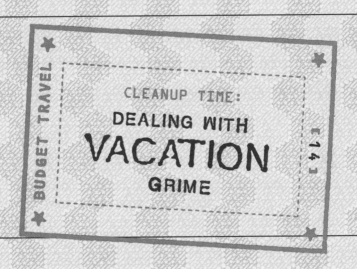

BUDGET TRAVEL

CLEANUP TIME:

DEALING WITH

VACATION

GRIME

[14]

WE'VE BIN THERE If you need a plastic bag for a wet swimsuit or dirty diapers, look in the bottom of your hotel trash can. Housekeepers often tuck in extra bags.

DeDe O'Connor, Cambria, Calif.

A DIRTY TRICK On family trips, we each bring our own roller suitcase and pack a pop-up laundry basket for everyone to use. During vacation, all the dirty clothes go into the basket. When it's time to head home, we put them all in one suitcase.

Eileen Lyon, Encino, Calif.

SPRINKLE SOME SUDS Here's a great way to pack powdered detergent for washing clothes in a sink: Clean out one of those plastic spice containers that have a shaker cap and fill it with detergent. When you're ready to wash clothes, just shake a little powder into the sink.

Joan Burns, Silver Spring, Md.

BREAD HEELS Save your bags of store-bought bread—they're perfect for packing kids' shoes. The dirt on the sneakers won't get all over everything else in the suitcase.

Melanie Martin, Huntsville, Ala.

A DRY IDEA For my Costa Rican vacation, I brought a small dry bag (the kind commonly used on rafting and kayaking trips) to store damp clothes. And because it's completely watertight, it also doubled as a laundry washbasin!

Julie de Jesus, Flagstaff, Ariz.

GAG PRIZE Plastic grocery bags are handy for lots of different travel mishaps. I roll one up tightly and store it inside a film canister. When my 7-year-old daughter and I went to an IMAX show that featured lots of swooping mountain shots, I had my canister in hand—just in case.

Diane Atwood, Cumberland, Maine

A DAB WILL DO<<<<<<<<<<<<<

Since it's important to tackle stains quickly, I travel with a Tide to Go stick tucked in my purse. About the size of a ballpoint pen, it works wonders when we're on the road. And it's cheaper than using the hotel laundry.

Vikki Kristic, Ferndale, Calif.

NAVY SECRET<<<<<<<<<<<<

Place a fabric-softener sheet in your suitcase when packing. It'll absorb odors and dampness and keep clothing smelling fresh. It's most beneficial in warm, humid climates and while at sea, as I learned while in the Navy.

Edward Jewell, Washington, D.C.

BABY YOURSELF Baby wipes aren't just for infants. Slip a travel-size pack into your carry-on bag and use the wipes to kill germs on public toilet seats and in phone booths. In a pinch, they can also remove stains from clothing.

Farrah Farhang, Fremont, Calif.

ALMOST LIKE WASHING I put bars of soap in various parts of our bags, including our laundry bag. They make everything smell better (and often come in handy).

Thomas Hank, Baker City, Ore.

BYOTP A quarter of a roll of toilet paper with a squashed tube fits nicely into a sandwich-size plastic bag, where it'll stay clean and tidy. Tuck it into a corner of your purse, camera bag, or carry-on, and it'll be available for on-the-road pit stops.

Alan Sweitzer, Kalamazoo, Mich.

MINIMIZE YOUR LAUNDRY Hotels that offer dry-cleaning or laundry service usually provide guests with plastic drawstring bags for dirty clothes. These are ideal for hauling your laundry home. Simply fill the bag, put it on the bed, and sit on it. Your body weight will force out all the air, and then your dirty clothes will take up almost no space in your luggage.

Lori Bremner, Sonoma, Calif.

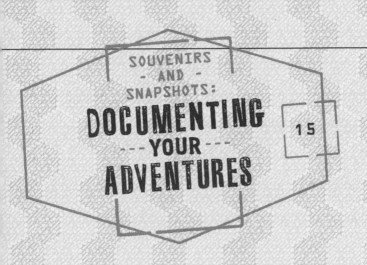

CHAPTER FIFTEEN

SOUVENIRS
- AND -
SNAPSHOTS:
DOCUMENTING
--- YOUR ---
ADVENTURES

15

LOCATION SHOOT Before my family goes on vacation, I always seek out a local photographer in our destination. Then, toward the end of our trip, we get our family photos taken. They really beat the typical studio photos and ensure great memories.

Jennifer Szarejko, Macomb, Mich.

NO STAMPS NECESSARY We figured out how to get our kids to keep journals. Each day they choose a postcard, and in the evening they write a few sentences about their adventures. We put the postcards on their own key ring. Instant souvenir flip books!

Chris Ignasiak, Avon, Ohio

PLACE MATS Kid-oriented destinations, such as Legoland and SeaWorld, often provide free paper maps of the parks. Instead of throwing them away, have them laminated and use them as placemats or decorations in your child's room.

Mike and Cindy Shields, Wellsville, Kans.

MUSICAL JOURNEY I purchase a couple of CDs on every international trip. Not the folk music you find in most tourist shops (which I rarely like), but some kind of local pop or rock. Unlike other souvenirs, the albums don't collect dust because we play them over and over, bringing back memories of all the places we've been.

John F. Woodward, Ames, Iowa

O KEY-CHAIN TREE Our kids like to bring home Christmas-tree decorations as souvenirs, but if it's not the right season, we can't always find what we want. We now steer the kids to key-chain racks. When we get home, we remove the key rings, tie on a pretty piece of ribbon, and voilà, instant ornament. Postcards and ticket stubs work well, too!

Laura and Ron Barak, Deerfield Beach, Fla.

WINNING SHOT When our kids were younger, we gave them disposable cameras and held photo contests on family trips. We'd come up with different "best photo" categories—of a meal, a seashell, a sunset, etc.—and hand out awards at the end of the vacation.

Wendy VanHatten, Sergeant Bluff, Iowa

PAPER TRAIL For each of our European vacations, we make a scrapbook that includes menus, receipts, tickets, and postcards. We've also found that outdated guidebooks, as well as old travel magazines, are a great source of maps, pictures, and commentaries on the places we've visited. We cut them up and stash them in a folder we pick up before the trip.

Henry and Carolyn Heitmann,
Fort Myers Beach, Fla.

PENNY WISE My 8-year-old collects smashed pennies, those souvenir coins that are run through a press and imprinted with a design. Turns out that the Web site pennycollector.com lists all the coin-smashing machines around the country and even worldwide. My son logs on, finds the machines near our destination, and is instantly fascinated by wherever we're going.

Cynthia Turner, Seattle, Wash.

SNAPFISH TO SNAP FISH We planned on doing a lot of snorkeling while in Hawaii, so I bought disposable underwater cameras on the mainland, where they are less expensive. I also picked up prepaid mailing envelopes from a photo developer (Snapfish, in my case). Once finished with the cameras, I dropped them in the mail, and the pictures were waiting for us when we got home.

Christine Zardecki, Highland Park, N.J.

MEET IN THE MIDDLE On vacations, my husband and I share a travel journal. One of us records thoughts, observations, and experiences, starting at the front of the journal, and the other starts writing from the back. We don't read what the other has written until we get home. This has given us surprises, laughs, and insights into how at times we see things quite differently.

Glenna Simms, Wheat Ridge, Colo.

PATTERN PLAY Before big family trips, I always buy a yard of colorful fabric. It makes a festive tablecloth or picnic blanket during our travels. I found a print with zebras for a trip to Africa and one with lizards for Costa Rica. Back home, I glue a piece of the fabric to the front of our vacation album, which makes it easy to spot and brings back good memories.

Janeen McAllister, St. Paul, Minn.

COLLECTIVE MEMORY I recently discovered journals from a 1927 trip my family took to Europe and Palestine. There were entries from three generations—it was fascinating to read each person's account. I now try to encourage every member of a group trip to contribute to a journal.

Joan White, Dallas, Tex.

WRAP STAR When we travel, I look for wrapping paper in regional designs. While in Australia, I found paper with koalas and kangaroos. In Hawaii, I got paper decorated with surfers and hula dancers. Gifts for the folks back home mean even more when they're wrapped in paper that you can't buy just anywhere.

Betsy Rogers, Puyallup, Wash.

JOURNAL JUMP START Before we went to London, I created a personalized booklet on our computer with fill-in pages like "the new foods I tried were," "best candy," "words I learned," and "most fun/boring museums." My daughter had a blast answering the questions and filling in all the details.

Mary Cronin, Harwich, Mass.

A TASTE OF THE WORLD Instead of bringing back cheap souvenirs for friends, we buy a cookbook with recipes native to the place we're visiting. When we get home, we host a cultural dinner at which we share our pictures and make some dishes from the cookbook. Our friends and family tell us that they prefer the meals because, unlike throwaway souvenirs, the memories of the dinners last forever.

Sarah J. Latchaw, Lawrenceville, Ga.

LOOK BOOK We keep a handy little notebook in which we record every trip we've taken, whether by car, plane, train, or boat. Each trip description begins with the destination and the dates traveled, as well as stops for gas and food, highway numbers, motels (with costs), and any interesting sights we saw along the way. We have found this to be most helpful in remembering what happened, when, and where. We started in 1970 and are now on our fourth book. We've even made an index of the places we've traveled and the date, with the page number of the specific book, which saves us time when we're trying to look something up.

Phyllis S. Dixon, Rapid City, S.D.

FAMILY FOOTAGE On vacations, we always let the kids use our Flip camcorder. Flips are relatively inexpensive and easy to use. We download the videos nightly, delete what we don't like, and, using built-in FlipShare software, make our own movies that we post on our Web site. They have a big following with our friends and family!

Steve Senn, Colorado Springs, Colo.

IT'S A WRAP On a recent trip to Italy, we picked up an Italian newspaper to use as fun and inexpensive wrapping paper. We even matched the section of the paper with the recipient, using colorful photos of soccer players to wrap a gift for a soccer-playing relative. We found that family members took as much interest in the wrapping paper as they did in the gift!

Ruth Schnur, Princeton, N.J.

ABOUT THE AUTHOR—IT'S YOU! If *Budget Travel* runs your tip in the magazine, you'll receive a one-year subscription. E-mail it to Tips@BudgetTravel.com, and remember to include your mailing address.

If you'd like to subscribe to *Budget Travel*—where you'll find new tips from real travelers in every issue—you can do so at BudgetTravel.com.

The 350 tips in this book all came from readers of *Budget Travel*. Margot Guralnick combed through and compiled them from the thousands you've shared over the years, so keep 'em coming.

The book was checked for accuracy by Yelena Moroz and copyedited by Molly Powell. The tips were updated before going to press. If you see an inaccuracy, please let us know at the above e-mail address.

Budget Travel would also like to thank the smart, talented designers and editors at Quirk Books. It's safe to say that without them, this book wouldn't be as delightful as it is.